# The Devil,
# Delfina Varela
# & the Used Chevy

# The Devil, Delfina Varela & the Used Chevy

(**W**hich examines Delfina Varela's puzzling pact with the Devil, the plaintive love story of Ruiz Lopez Mondragon, and the doomed Hispanic political dream of Manuel Caballo**s**)

# Louie García Robinson

ANCHOR BOOKS
New York   London   Toronto   Sydney   Auckland

An Anchor Book

PUBLISHED BY DOUBLEDAY

a division of Bantam Doubleday Dell Publishing Group, Inc.
1540 Broadway, New York, New York 10036

ANCHOR BOOKS, DOUBLEDAY, and the portrayal of an anchor
are trademarks of Doubleday,
a division of Bantam Doubleday Dell Publishing Group, Inc.

ACKNOWLEDGMENT:

I wish to thank Charles Conrad, Senior Editor at Anchor Books, for providing
editorial direction and numerous sound suggestions; above all for his patience
and sense of humor in taming a preposterous and unrestrained original
manuscript.

PHOTO CREDITS:

TIB West/Pete Turner (P. 1); TIB West/Chuck Fishman (P. 7); TIB West/Paolo
Curto (P. 17); TIB West/Michael Salas (P. 51); TIB West/Jay Fries (P. 63);
Louie G. Robinson (P. 151); TIB West/G & J Images, Inc. (P. 165); TIB
West/Nanci Brown (left), Larry Gordon (right) (P. 171); Bettmann (P. 189);
Louie G. Robinson (P. 195); TIB West/Pete Turner (P. 247); TIB West/Pete
Turner (P. 283)

Library of Congress Cataloging-in-Publication Data

Robinson, Louie García.
The Devil, Delfina Varela & the used Chevy : which examines Delfina Varela's
puzzling pact with the Devil, the plaintive love story of Ruiz Lopez Mondragon,
and the doomed Hispanic political dream of Manuel Caballos / Louie García
Robinson. — 1st. ed.
  p.    cm.
I. Title.   II. Title: Devil, Delfina Varela, and the used Chevy.
PS3568.O31226D48   1993
813'.54—dc20                                                 93-12693
                                                                  CIP

ISBN 0-385-46868-7

Book Design by Gretchen Achilles

Printed in the United States of America
Anchor Books Paperback Original

First Edition: September 1993

3   5   7   9   10   8   6   4

# Dedication

To the Real Delfina Varela,
my mother, Sara García Montes.

*Along a Parabola*
*Life like rocket flies,*
*Mainly in darkness,*
*Now and then on a*
*Rainbow*
        Andre Voznesensky


*The most beautiful thing we can experience is the mysterious.*
*It is the source of all true art and science.*
        Albert Einstein


*Good humor is goodness and wisdom combined.*
        Fortune cookie message


*God is fat.*
        Jorge Amado

# Las Señoritas Lucrecia y Dolores

Metichis. Gossips.

# Prologue

"Are you going to Judge Abelardo Quintana's wedding, dear?" asked that terrible gossip and busybody, Señorita Dolores.

"But of course, *querida*," replied her gossiping co-conspirator, Señorita Lucrecia. "There will be enough there to talk about for years to come."

"But, tell me, what could a respected man like Judge Quintana see in that poor thing, Esmeralda Lopez?"

"*¿Quién sabe?*"

"Can you understand men?"

"Only God can understand them."

"And even He has doubts."

"The judge is a prince among men."

"A self-made man."

"Attended law school while working at Sears."

"While his mother had cancer."

"No, dear, I think it was emphysema."

"Whatever. She used to smoke."

"Camels."

"No, *querida*, I think it was Marlboros."

"You are right. It was Marlboros. Marlboro Lights."

"I know I am right. Did you know he started his own law firm?"

"Yes, and then became a big shot in the law association and was named to the Port Commission."

"Founded a Chicano scholarship fund."

"*Mira nomas.* He has always cared for his people. But she? *¿Qué?* What has she done? *Nada.*"

"She is okay."

"For a child, poor thing."

"How old is she?"

"Why she's just barely out of high school. I think she is eighteen."

"No, dear, I think she is nineteen."

"No, she is eighteen."

"No, dear, she graduated last September. *Uno, dos, tres, quatro* . . . She would be nineteen now. Don't you see?"

"*Ya que,* whatever."

"But look at her, marrying Judge Abelardo Quintana."

"She won the *premio gordo* the first time she played the Lotto."

"*Mira nomas.*"

"From the playground to the high ground."

"Kind of pretty."

"But lots of baby fat."

"Too young."

"Too young and too fat."

"Secretary in a law office."

"No, dear, a file clerk."

"*¿No me lo digas?* Is that right?"

"Yes. And poor? *Oo-joo-le.*"

"*Aiii cállate.* Poor as a beggar. She is probably after his money."

"Of course. What else? But, you know, he still has the twinkle in his eyes. *¿No piensas?*"

"Of course. Any fool can see that. Men will sacrifice

everything for some young thigh. Everything. Even if they're fat."

"But why?"

"Only God knows. I think it makes them feel young. *¿No piensas?*"

"How should I know? Before his wife died . . ."

"A wonderful, wonderful woman . . ."

"Wonderful woman. She must be a saint in Heaven by now. But, you know, before she died, there was talk of his hanky-panky. Somebody told me that he had other girl friends."

"Well? What would you expect?"

"Men are all the same."

"Men are all the same."

Señorita Lucrecia and Señorita Dolores stopped briefly to catch their breath. Lucrecia poured Dolores a cup of tea.

"I hear the wedding ceremony will be very big."

"That's what I heard."

"I hope Pelon doesn't cry."

"He will."

"Are you going to the reception?"

"But, of course."

"Me too. From what I hear there will be lots of music."

"Shark Salazar and Los Falcones will play the music."

"*¡Hijo!* He's good."

"The best."

"Are you going to try to dance?"

"*¿Quién sabe?* Don't you think I can? Why wouldn't I? I am not dead yet. I am not a cripple."

"I didn't say that."

"But you meant it."

"No I didn't."

"*Ya que.*"

"There will be lots of music and lots of food."

"Lots of music and lots of food and lots of hooch."

"*¿Qué quiere decir* 'hooch'?"

"*Licor.*"

"*Ah, vaya, licor.* They will need lots of hooch for Father *In*Clemente and Conde Pacheco and those other *borrachentos.*"

"I bet Esmeralda's brother, Ruy Lopez, gets drunk. You want to bet? Come on, bet me."

"Of course not. He *will* get drunk. He will get drunk and stupid. You can set your watch by it."

"They say the Mayor may show up."

"*¿No me lo digas?*"

"*Sí.* And there's a rumor that Linda Ronstadt may show up and sing, maybe."

"No? *¡Qué cosa!* You are just making that up."

"I don't know where I heard it, and it is not a 'for sure.' It was just a rumor I heard someplace. Maybe she will show up and maybe she will not show up. How do I know?"

"*¿Qué rumor y qué papas?* You just made that up."

"This is going to be big."

"You are changing the subject but I agree. This is going to be *very* big."

"*Claro.* It will be one of the biggest things ever seen in *La Michon.*"

"*Sin duda,*" affirmed Señorita Lucrecia, "without a doubt."

# Delfina Varela

"Why do I keep asking for forgiveness?
For what?"

# 1. La Michon

Suddenly startled, several pigeons flap into flight as a gangly, shirtless youth with a sunken chest and long hair clatters by on a skateboard.

A man toting so many balloons he appears to be airborne walks past an affront of graffiti that proclaims "U.S. out of my UteruS."

Trying to look *so* cool, *so* tough, a Hispanic boy walks by wearing black, baggy pants, a white T-shirt that bears the image of *La Virgen de Guadalupe,* a black jacket, high-topped athletic shoes and a backward-facing L.A. Raiders cap; he's wearing the uniform of *La Michon.*

*La Michon* is as far from Eden as one can get, yet it's located in the middle of a metropolis named after St. Francis of Assisi that the locals call "the City" and that is known elsewhere as San Francisco.

*La Michon,* the Mission District, is the city's Hispanic zone, an area that abounds in sensual extremes. One has but to look across at an attractive young woman with short blond hair wearing white tights and a loose, oversized tan sweater that reveals a white shoulder as she skates by on a pair of chartreuse Roller Blades. She creates a wake of admiration that includes a toothless smile on the weathered face of an old man wearing a stained hat and a shiny suit.

A drunken black woman panhandles "for my kids," as a

hustler shows a tourist a watch that "ain't hot; if you know what I mean."

As a friend takes their photograph, girls in Catholic school uniforms giggle and squeal, their smiles trapped in metallic braces, as across the street, intellectuals, artists and poets mix with demimonde characters at the Café la Bohème.

Dizzying patterns, busy designs and bright colors predominate in *La Michon* as, on the corner of Mission and Twenty-fourth streets, an overwhelmed tourist appears bedazzled and frightened. He hails a cab to rescue him from this bewildering excess and return him to the relative safety of a Union Square hotel and the comfort of a Scotch on the rocks.

Manioc tubers, jicama, orange and green mangoes; orange papayas, tomatoes, avocados with the skins of alligators; hanging clusters of yellow bananas and small brown plantains are displayed in *La Michon* vegetable and fruit stands.

Little girls' pink, white and blue organza dresses are sold in shops where multicolored *piñatas* shaped like donkeys or stars or lizards hang from the ceiling and where shelves are lined with orange, blue and purple wigs.

A crucifix that glows in the dark is displayed in a store window next to a gigantic rosary with strands of inch-wide beads coiled around the base of a plaster Irish setter.

Completing this visual extravagance are red and blue tiles on Mission Street sidewalks, and walls covered with exotic, vivid murals depicting warriors or saints with gigantic, anguished faces.

Only in the quiet, early dawn can one hear the sound of distant church bells and an occasional passing Bay Area Rapid Transit train that rumbles under foot like a small earthquake; for as the day awakens in *La Michon* this quietness yields.

Buses and motorcycles choke the District's narrow streets, car horns blare at both friend and encroacher, and police cars, ambulances and fire trucks scream out a daily chorus of private misery. And the chattering, the constant chattering: vendors selling their wares, ice cream cart pushers playing their chimes and elaborately describing the attributes of their Popsicles; now and then, an occasional "Yo, bro'. ¿Qué pasa?" as well as mothers, in their constant vigil, yelling at children, "Carlos, be careful, mijito."

But, towering supreme over all of this cacophony is the lowrider "boom" car, low-slung automobiles that roll by very slowly, their drivers hidden behind tinted windows and mirror-lensed glasses, as powerful hi-tech speakers play a bass beat that is so intense it can be felt in the chest and diaphragm. These vehicles are the true chariots of sound in *La Michon.*

Much more subtle, but as pervasive, are the smells: the delicious aromas of *carnitas,* chicken in *mole* sauce, cooked tongue and other fillings that will go into burritos, enchiladas and tamales in countless District restaurants and *taquerías.* These aromas, which sweep across *La Michon,* blend with the smell of corn mash in lye that will be flattened and stamped into tortillas and the bouquet of chili peppers of every variety.

Competing with this is the stink of putrescence and decay and auto fumes and cheap colognes and toilet water as well as tired bars exuding the stench of stale liquor, cigarette smoke, urine and hopelessness.

But on this day it would be the sweet fragrance of incense, beeswax, furniture polish and flowers that would greet Delfina Varela as she entered *La Michon*'s Basilica of Mission Dolores, the spiritual heart of the Mission District at Dolores and Sixteenth streets. She was there to attend the wedding of Judge Abelardo Quintana and nineteen-year-old Esmeralda Lopez.

The short, stout Delfina walked with a slight rolling gait that favored her left foot. By her movement she appeared to be much older than her fifty-two years. Her severe dark clothing, complete with a black lace mantilla, made her appear to be in everlasting mourning. She dipped her right hand into the marble holy water font and made the sign of the cross by touching the tip of her thumb and crossed index finger to her forehead, chin and left and right cheek and then again to her forehead, stomach and left and right shoulder.

For Delfina Varela this would prove to be an unbelievable day; a day that would begin with the questioning of her Catholic beliefs and that would end several weeks later in a pact with the Devil. Can you possibly believe it? In fact, to tell the truth, and of course we must, Delfina came to her incredible religious rebellion right there in the middle of Judge Quintana's wedding, between the Kyrie Eleison and the moment the bald Pelon, who always seemed to be wallowing in sentimentality, began to cry like a baby.

But, can you imagine? Delfina Varela wanting to sell her soul to the Devil? She guessed she could get something for it. What she needed was a car and what she wanted was a *Cadiyác,* but she figured that at her age she would probably have to settle for a Chevrolet, perhaps even a used one. But then she had no idea what one could get for a soul, new or used. It had come to her, as they say, out of the blue, right there, in the middle of Judge Quintana's garish wedding. She was passing the olive pit rosary beads through her fingers, dutifully saying her Hail Marys and her Our Fathers. She was also staring at a holy picture of a crucified Jesus Christ—a scene that was vivid in detail and showed jet-black nails inserted into white palms and feet; waxy maroon emerged from wounds at the hands and feet, and from an awful gaping wound at the chest. More shiny blood flowed from a thorn-pierced forehead. And at the foot of the cross, looking up at her Dying Son, was a mourning Blessed Virgin Mary, the Mother of God.

"My sins have done this to you, O Jesus," whispered Delfina. She ran her fingers over the rosary beads, continuing her prayer.

". . . *Santa María, Madre de Dios, ruega por nosotros los pecadores, ahora y en la hora de nuestra muerte. Amén.*"

Delfina had repeated the words to the Hail Mary thousands of times. But, for some reason, it was as if she were listening to them for the very first time. Delfina repeated the prayer very slowly, this time in English.

". . . Holy Mary, Mother of God, pray for us sinners, now and at the hour of our death. Amen."

Delfina stared at the gory picture of the crucifixion scene curiously, for a very long time. She exhaled deeply.

And then it happened. Something clicked. A little nerve somewhere in her head short-circuited.

"*¿Ya que?* What sinners? What sins?" asked Delfina out loud.

"Shhhh . . ."

"*Cht, cht . . .*"

Delfina bowed her head, began to whisper. "I never have any fun anymore. I never commit sins. Why do I keep asking for forgiveness? For what? I have not even had a man in eight years and I have not missed Sunday mass since I went to the funeral of my Tío Clotildo in Albuquerque in 1968."

Those in the pew beside her quickly turned to her, "Shhhhh."

Delfina Varela gathered her rosary beads and dropped them into her handbag, the pretty one from Mexico made out of iguana leather. She then turned to those hushing her and called out, *"Estúpidos."*

And that is the way Delfina Varela's rebellion began. Can you imagine? Right there in the middle of Judge Abelardo Quintana's lovely wedding.

We will, of course, examine all of this in some detail, as well as the strategies employed by Delfina in attempting to sell her soul to the Devil for a *Cadiyác,* preferably a new one. We do this not out of a morbid curiosity—we will leave that to historians, sociologists and those two *metichis,* those two nosy busybodies, Señorita Dolores and Señorita Lucrecia. Rather we do so to deter others who may be contemplating the same kind of deal, but who instead may end up in the same kind of pickle.

We will examine the way the Devil, in the person of a handsome young man in baggy pants, finally appeared to relieve Delfina of much more than her anxieties; a person who also involved Delfina's humble Mission District home in a spectacular shoot-out with the police of the City and County of San Francisco and the California Highway Patrol.

Needless to say, we will also go into exacting, almost lurid, detail in describing the Great Love Story involving Ruiz Lopez Mondragon and a mysterious, spectacular chimera. Interwoven will be the everlasting search by a Hispanic dreamer and political activist for a Mexican John F. Kennedy, as well as the terrible fate of . . .

But, wait. Wait a minute! One thing at a time.

As for the Wedding of Judge Quintana and Esmeralda Lopez . . .

# The "Twin Marías" Quintana

María Elena and María Christina were unhappy with their new stepmother. She was too young, too fat, too ugly.

# 2. The Wedding

The Basilica of Mission Dolores was filled with lilies and roses and gladioli as a setting sun filled the church with a sad orange glow. Iridescent saints, angels and other deities looked down sternly from stained-glass windows. There were candles and incense and eight bridesmaids dressed in mint green dresses and men dressed in shiny aqua-blue tuxedos and blue patent leather shoes.

"Breathtaking, simply breathtaking," whispered that old *metichi*, Señorita Lucrecia. She was whispering to her good friend and fellow gossip, Señorita Dolores.

The organ began to play. The doors of the church opened and the bride walked slowly into church accompanied by her father.

Señorita Dolores cupped her hand, conspiracy-style, "She's *such* a big girl. The bridal gown looks like a white muumuu."

"*Ai.* Dolores, *chhhhhh,* be still," said Lucrecia, smiling.

"Look at that thing she's carrying."

The bridal bouquet consisted of gladioli surrounded by ferns. "It looks like she is carrying a tree," said Señorita Lucrecia.

Señorita Dolores elaborated. "If someone tries to catch that thing they will be killed."

Delfina Varela, who was sitting behind the two gossips, had had enough. "*Chhhh.* Can't you two be quiet?"

Señorita Lucrecia turned to give Delfina a withering look. *"Mira nomas.* St. Delfina Varela."

*"Aii, tu,"* said Señorita Dolores throwing her head up, greatly offended.

The ring bearer Eufemio Galian came into view. Ten-year-old Eufemio was growing up to be a midget. He was hardly three feet in height. With his pomaded hair, blue bow tie, tailor-made tuxedo and patent leather shoes, he resembled a shiny, dark doll. The red velvet cushion on which he carried the rings for the ceremony was almost too big and only served to emphasize his dwarfism. But he managed to walk down the main church aisle with dignity and bearing even though he had to look over the top of the cushion to see where the hell he was going.

It was a spectacle of overwhelming proportions: a Mexican wedding, a thundering organ, the cloying smell of incense mixed with the aroma of beeswax and the fragrance of reeking flowers. The Basilica walls, statues and mosaic images seemed to join the singers in the choir loft shouting down the communion of saints, the forgiveness of sins and the power of the Most Blessed Trinity: God the Father, God the Son and, most mysterious of all, God the Holy Ghost—the Little God, the one that looks like a little pigeon with a halo and a tongue of orange flame shooting out of its head.

*"Mira.* Look at the Twin Marías," said Señorita Dolores.

"They are ready to cry," said Señorita Lucrecia.

"Can you blame them?"

Two of the bridesmaids were the groom's daughters, the Twin Marías: María Elena and María Cristina. The Judge's nineteen-year-old daughters were slender and fair and graceful, a marked contrast to the bride's darkness and roundness.

Of the hundreds of photographs taken at the wedding, several would show Judge Quintana's daughters looking scornfully in the direction of the bride. The Twin Marías were unhappy with their new stepmother. She was too young, too fat, too ugly. She was immature, giggly and, the worst sin of all, loud. Her good friends were Teresita and Rosalinda, Terry and Rosy, secretaries in a Mission Street law office. Later, at the wedding reception, Esmeralda and her two good friends would giggle endlessly. Perhaps, the Quintana sisters reasoned, Father would get over his silliness. Their new "mother." The word was like a fish bone in the throat. Who was she anyway? What did she want? What could a distinguished man like Father see in this . . . this thing, this dark beast with the mind of a child and the body of a hippopotamus?

The lovely, twin Quintana sisters ached with melancholy. It had taken their father a long time to get over the sudden death of their mother, a clever, handsome, cultivated woman. A period of dark sadness had followed. Long walks accompanied periods of meaningless activity. Their father had stayed away from the house for weeks at a time, unable to face the monotony, the daily tedium of life. Until one day, finally, his sadness yielded. It was over when he decided to sell their huge home and move into a bright, sun-filled condominium on Potrero Hill, the City's "sun belt" with views of both the Bay and the City. There had followed a series of relationships with elegant ladies who were invariably sparkling and witty. All had been amusing and clever—women with law degrees or interesting occupations in marketing or public relations or other professions. Smart, handsome women, the kind who added to Father's standing and dignity and who would add immeasurably to his legal prestige.

One, Grace McKenzie, a psychiatrist who played the harpsichord, was particularly appealing. She was a beautiful lady who always brought gifts and even, on occasion, had sung to them. She had studied the history of Spain and could relate wonderful stories of Iberia, of the Moorish Occupation, of ʿAbd-al-Rahmān III, of the spectacular beauty of the Alhambra in Granada or the Alcázar in Seville or the Gaudi architecture in Barcelona. And her Spanish, though pleasantly accented, was perfect. One evening, after clearing the dishes following a triumphant dinner in which Grace—even the name was perfect—had charmed them thoroughly, María Elena whispered to her sister in the kitchen, "That's the one. She's going to be our new stepmother."

"Oh, God, wouldn't that be wonderful," sighed María Cristina breathlessly. The two sisters hugged each other. Had they not been within earshot they would have squealed gleefully.

But their father had not chosen Grace McKenzie, despite those beautiful notes in her lovely handwriting. He had chosen the young Esmeralda Lopez instead, an all-too-young law clerk their father had known for but a month before proposing to her. The wedding pictures would clearly show the sadness in the eyes of the beautiful María Elena and María Cristina as they looked at their new stepmother/child, Esmeralda.

So be it. The Twin Marías conceded that it was the Will of God.

Exquisite Byzantine patterns, hypnotic in appeal, cast a spell of mosaic, geometric puzzles on the church walls, and from a daydream of stars, the bride's brother, Ruy Lopez, emerged, first to the Basilica of Mission Dolores and then to the ceremony—that breathtaking ceremony—and then to his wife, Amapola, his fat, brown wife who was sitting next to him and who smelled of lilacs. How dreamy, how abstract: the tiled patterns, the sweet aromas, the flickering candles, the expiring orange sunlight mixing with the first evening star, the stained-glass windows, the massive wooden pews that smelled of furniture polish. Ruy looked around. The topmost level of large stained-glass windows, which usually rained down a fiery red/orange glow (a reminder of Hell?), were now muted by the evening light. Below that, in a second row of stained-glass windows, Santa Barbara, San Rafael, San Diego, Santa Clara, San Fernando and other saints showered rays of light onto the California missions that bore their names. Behind an iron grill, St. Theresa was holding a bouquet of allergy-inducing flowers, and, at a small side altar, a white statue of the Sacred Heart of Jesus was surrounded by three walls covered with an endless series of crosses rendered in mosaic tile. Bowing his head reverently, Ruy was almost overwhelmed by the power and majesty of faith and ceremony. How very sensual. How lovely. How strange.

The stocky thirty-two-year-old Ruy Lopez was a happy, handsome man: cinnamon complexion, jet-black hair, thick lips, and, "miracle of miracles"—his mother's words—he had blue eyes. He felt constrained wearing a suit and tie, although he wore them well. He smiled. His gardening business was going well. His wife was loyal and his mistress, Mrs. Winifred Lampson Birdwell, although "a bit off-center," was accessible and not very demanding. So she *was* "a lady of a certain age" as she put it whenever he asked her age, she *did* own a house in Pacific Heights, one of the most exclusive sections of San Francisco. The sprawling mansion overlooked the entire San Francisco Bay from the Golden Gate Bridge and Tiburon to southern Oakland, and had the biggest garden on his entire route.

And now his little sister, Esmeralda, scarcely nineteen years old, was marrying Judge Abelardo Quintana, a great man. Ruy could almost weep with happiness. What did it matter that the judge was three times as old as Esmeralda? They were in love. Besides, if anything went wrong, she would be financially set. Ruy turned to look at his brother, Victor, who was serving as an usher. Good looking, ambitious, his little brother was becoming a respected lawyer. He also headed a grass-roots lawyer's group whose aim was to force the gerrymandering of voting districts according to ethnic voting blocks. Victor's affiliation was bringing about truly meaningful change. He was on his way to becoming a community leader and some were even talking about Victor as a potential politician. What a guy! What a family! Ruy sighed. It was all so pretty, so perfect. Later on he would sip a tequila and bite down hard into a thick, juicy lime. He could almost feel the sourness bursting into his mouth. Ruy swallowed.

Elsewhere in the Basilica, in a forward pew, was five-year-old Angelina Maestras, a small white doll with an angelic face and perfect, dainty lips. She wore a white dress with ribbons and lace, and a pair of gold, loop earrings in her pierced ears. She turned slowly to the back of the church to look up to the choir loft, up above the marble holy water fonts and the mosaic tile image of the *Virgen de Guadalupe,* up above the wood carving of the Holy Family, up to the choral singers shrieking of blood and death and eternal damnation. When he saw her perfect face, Ruy was filled with an intense Hispanic pride. There in Angelina was the future, a bright Hispanic future. Angelina, so splendid a child, a marvel to behold: with her small perfect lips and delicate nose and deep dark eyes and glistening earrings in her pierced ears. In the very middle of Ruy's small, golden hope, Angelina proudly picked her nose and extracted a shiny pearl that she studied with great curiosity before wiping it on her pretty white dress.

Lying on his back, in the middle aisle, was Angelina's three-year-old brother, Sergio. He was looking at the saints and angels on the church walls, at the stern figures of the Twelve Apostles encased in round gold frames. But he was most interested in the mosaic tile patterns on the walls. He traced the line of intricate angles with his index finger following their complex formations. He began making noises, of cars and trucks, and the patterns around him turned into a maze of streets and highways and freeways.

"Brrrrrrr . . ." Sky cars would turn into sky trucks and then into helicopters and erratic airplanes and these in turn would change into giant bees ("Zzzzzzzzz . . .") flying in precise angled patterns traced by Sergio on the church walls. The bees flew across a blue, pastel sky, past billowing, white clouds and across the faces of the archangels, St. Michael, St. Raphael and St. Gabriel. The bees turned into spaceships filled with passengers that hovered near a lamp filled with small rainbows and control rooms. The spaceship turned into a space station that suddenly went out of control and dropped to earth and exploded violently as Sergio's hand slapped the tan aisle carpet on which he was lying. It was a dramatic, incredible crash, "Fweeeeeeee-Keeeroooobratrch" which created a million flaming pieces which, of course, only Sergio could see.

"Sergio, what are you doing?" asked Angelina, as Sergio's hand turned into a submarine sailing down, down through a silent undersea world.

"Nothing. Whishsssss."

In an adjacent pew sat Mateo Figueroa, wiping the perspiration from his face with an oversized blue handkerchief. Mateo was perpetually grief-stricken, a tortured saint in a painting by El Greco. Next to Mateo sat his small, obedient wife, Lupe. A patch of yellow, reflected light lay like an egg yolk across the exposed tops of her thick, brown breasts. Beside her, in a neat row, sitting according to age, were the Figueroa children—four boys and three girls—all with the same drooping eyes, a legacy of their sad father. The Figueroa family appeared to be in perpetual mourning, and, of course, they were.

Behind the Figueroa family sat Señorita Lucrecia. She was contemplating an interesting irony. How strange, she thought, that the very light-complected Pepe de la Vega and his almost blond wife, Marisa, had given birth to a baby who was fat and dark as a cockroach. Yet Tony and Leoparda de la O, who looked like Kickapoo Indians, had given birth to a child who resembled the little Baby Jesus in the Holy Picture Cards: blond, blue-eyed, white. How strange. Maybe the babies had been switched in the hospital. Señorita Lucrecia smiled. This was the stuff of rumor.

Meanwhile, Señorita Lucrecia's fellow meddler, Señorita Dolores, was contemplating an even richer vein of gossip. There before her was the gloriously pregnant Amalia Alegre. Look at her, brazen bitch, unmarried and pregnant. What more need be said? Wouldn't be surprised if she dropped calf right here, in the middle of the good Judge Quintana's wedding. Some hussies will do anything for attention. Who could the father be? The only ones who really cared were she and Señorita Lucrecia; not like the good old days when such a thing would have been considered a terrible scandal and young, unmarried pregnant girls were properly hidden away in homes for unwed mothers where they belonged. Look at her. Amalia Alegre glowed with the pride of pregnancy. She was so gay, so elated by her colossal fertility.

On that hot evening, in that warm church Bunny García, wearing oversized metal earrings that rattled every time she turned her head, was holding a tasseled Chinese fan. When Bunny saw that Señorita Lucrecia and Señorita Dolores were staring at her she snapped the Chinese fan open to reveal a scene of two red monkeys perched in a yellow banana tree and locked in an obscene embrace.

"Indecent," said Señorita Lucrecia, using her favorite word.

"Disgusting," said Señorita Dolores using hers.

Bunny looked at the two gossips and smiled. She had as much right to be here as anyone, for after all she had been invited to attend the wedding by none other than Esmeralda's sentimental father, Mauricio. If only she could tell those two awful gossips that the obscene fan she was waving at them had been given to her by Mauricio, who happened to be one of her most admiring and regular customers. He paid twice weekly visits, on Tuesday and Thursday, to the place where Bunny García worked, the Marisol Emporium of Psychic Counseling and Healing, a pretentious camouflage for one of the finest houses of prostitution in *La Michon*.

Bunny rolled up the sleeves of her dress to reveal the darkness of her arms and their black hair. All around her sat men and women exposing wide expanses of darkened skin. And amidst all of this darkness sat Ruy's mistress, Winifred Lampson Birdwell, with her fair skin and blond hair. Her thin white arms and neck, her high cheekbones and light complexion and honey-blond hair contrasted sharply with the roundnesses and darknesses and bright colors of those surrounding her.

To his mother's embarrassment, Sergio Maestras went up to Winifred Birdwell to inspect her face, her hands, her neck, the golden follicles of her arms. Finally, with great timidity, he reached over to touch her hand. He did so with reverence, as if touching the big toe of the statue of St. Francis. He had never seen anyone so white. She was like a glass of milk. He looked up to see the white lady's face and Winifred smiled and touched Sergio's hand with an expression of encompassing kindness. Had she been traveling she would have tenderly offered the boy money or tooth-decaying candy. Her gesture, which aroused such compassion in the woman, only succeeded in frightening Sergio, who fled to the safety of his mother's thick thigh and her solid, rancid smell.

Winifred Lampson Birdwell was observing the wedding with great curiosity: an anthropologist witnessing an exotic tribal ceremony. The bridesmaids in mint green, the men in blue tuxedos, the blaring windows, the priest who genuflected as if he were about to fall on his face, and the smells, the cloying smells: burning beeswax and incense mixed with the profuse aromas of flowers and toilet water. Next to Winifred Birdwell was her splendid daughter, Alexis, home for the summer following a junior year at the University of Salamanca. She too was observing everything, coyly aware of her mother's affair with Ruy Lopez, and the fact that Winifred Lampson Birdwell perceived this trip to this neighborhood and this church as a great, dangerous safari.

And then it happened. The other thing. One could hear it approaching like a truck in a tunnel. Everything in the church began shaking like Jell-O. People began to scream. The organ stopped. The church bells began to toll. Dogs began to bark.

"It is our final hour," screamed Señorita Lucrecia, crossing herself, preparing for her triumphant Entry into Heaven. "Get ready, Dolores, dear."

Angelina Maestras began to cry and then the Figueroa children, followed by Eufemio Galian. You would think they had never seen a little thing like a fatal, catastrophic earthquake before. The hanging lamps and banners began to sway like trapezes.

Ta-tatum-ta-ta . . . Ta-tatum-ta-ta . . .

*"Mierda santísima,"* said Ruy Lopez thinking that perhaps those would be his final, dying words.

"Down on your knees," screamed the priest, Father Clemente, ready to face Death with a flaming sword. As usual, Father Clemente had consumed too much sacramental wine. Because he was seldom sober, a blasphemous parish wag began calling him Father *"In*Clemente," a name that was so appropriate it stuck to the priest like Super Glue. Someone referring to "Father Clemente" would be met with a puzzled look. *"Ah, vaya,* you mean Father *In*Clemente."

The tipsy priest covered the backs of the bride and groom with his chasuble as he threw his hand in the direction of Danger, ready to shield Judge Quintana and Esmeralda

Lopez from a falling Corinthian column, which would have been difficult since there are no Corinthian columns in the Basilica of Mission Dolores.

Yet, as quickly as it started, the earthquake stopped.

Everyone felt relieved and a little shy to have been so frightened. Señorita Dolores and Señorita Lucrecia looked at each other stupidly. A reprieve from death is always a bit embarrassing.

Up at the altar Father *In*Clemente looked rather theatrical sheltering the bride and groom with his chasuble. Striking his pose, the priest resembled a saint in a prayer card. All that was missing were shafts of gold and pink light and fat-rumped baby angels holding baby harps descending from broken clouds.

"It must have been an earthquake," said Father *In*Clemente wiping his lips. His mouth felt very dry.

Ruy Lopez shook his head wondering what final words most people uttered right before they were killed: "Holy shit," "What did you call me?" "I'll show you, asshole!" "Holy Mother of God." "There is nothing to worry about. Please remain seated."

Kneeling next to Ruy was Manuel ("Manny") Caballos, a successful Mission District beer distributor. He bowed his head reverently to pray and wiped his face with a large red bandana and then folded his hands. He studied the scar on the back of his left hand. The scar marked the spot of a youthful indiscretion: the tattoo of a small cross that had been surgically removed. As a teenager in *Islos*—East Los Angeles—he had labored for hours with needle and ink to create the tattoo. It was his handsome daughter, the twenty-one-year-old Celine, who had asked him to have the tattoo removed. "Else,

*Papi,* you will never be taken seriously in your business and you will always appear like a cheap L.A. punk."

He had gotten angry with her; he had shouted at her and even menaced her, but afterwards, overcome with sorrow for abusing his beloved daughter, his most precious possession, he recanted and had the tattoo removed. When he showed her his bandaged hand she finally smiled for the first time in days. Celine, in her own way, had made her father remove the tattoo and Manny Caballos, in his own way, had capitulated to her to make amends for his terrible, uncontrollable temper. After that, nothing was said; nothing needed to be said. The tattoo was never mentioned again. It was as simple as that.

In the great Basilica of Mission Dolores, Father *In*Clemente hurried through the last part of the ceremony thinking of the reception, and, above all, the refreshments that would soon follow. He had just celebrated the Sacrifice of the Mass; he had performed the Sacrament of Matrimony and participated in Holy Communion. In the middle of the earthquake he was certain he would be adding to this list by administering the Last Rites. His mouth felt very dry. As he turned to the parishioners to give the final blessing signaling the end of the wedding mass, Angelina Maestras, still frightened by the earthquake, continued to cry and whine with a deep and sincere passion and a runny nose.

Outside the church, a number of dogs, the Catholic ones, could be heard barking, praying to God for the salvation of their immortal dog souls, not realizing that *all* dogs go to Heaven.

And that was the way, the unforgettable way the wedding of Judge Abelardo Quintana and Esmeralda Lopez ended. Amen.

# 3. The Reception

The tears would puddle in Señorita Lucrecia's eyes years later whenever she spoke of it. *"Ai, Dios mío,* unless you had been there you would not believe how pretty life could be."

She spoke of the wedding reception for Judge Abelardo Quintana and Esmeralda Lopez which took place in the Mission Dolores Parish Hall. For, on that starry night, there was singing and dancing; there were dogs and cats and laughter. There were aromas of food and perfume and cologne and Mexican cognac and cigars and cigarettes; and at the windows there were stars in a moonless night. There were good things to eat, including Rita Anaya's delicious raisin and cinnamon tamales, Señora Talavera's turkey in chocolate *mole* sauce and Bunny García's exquisite persimmon cookies, a recipe she had learned from her sister in Modesto. And when Ruy Lopez sank his teeth into one of Bunny García's fat persimmon cookies, he rolled his eyes toward Heaven and, as if witnessing a beatific vision, exclaimed, "Jesus Christ, this is unbelievable." He was not kidding. There was also some good Tecate beer and wine and a little of the hard stuff for the boozers like Judge Abelardo Quintana and Father *In*Clemente. And needless to say there was also champagne. Above all there was life itself: music and dancing.

The young girls were dazzling, aromatic bouquets of exotic flowers. They looked so fragile the boys hardly dared approach them. It was a graceful evening filled with pleasant sights and sounds, delicious food, affection and music. There were also dark children with shining eyes who thought the entire evening was an unbelievable adventure.

On the dance floor, couples laughed and turned as they danced to the salsa music of Los Falcones, a band led by Shark Salazar, a perspiring drummer with a terrible scar on his face and a bunny rabbit tattoo on his right hand.

The dancers stepped aside to give the newlyweds room to dance. The judge wore a white tuxedo and Esmeralda wore a white wedding gown with a veil. She had already kicked off her shoes, much to the chagrin of the Twin Marías.

Manny Caballos exclaimed, "You know, this isn't all that bad." And then, following a long sigh, he added, "Just think, a few minutes ago I was ready to croak." This just before he took out his dirty, red handkerchief and wiped his wet eyes and blew his nose. It wasn't that Caballos didn't have other handkerchiefs. He had dozens of handkerchiefs, drawers filled with handkerchiefs. People were always giving him handkerchiefs as gifts. Handkerchiefs for Christmas, for his birthday, for Father's Day. "Can't they ever think of anything else?" Fine linen handkerchiefs from the Orient; pure cotton, pastel-colored handkerchiefs from Belgium. The ones from France were even monogrammed. But it didn't matter. He preferred his large, red bandanas from the San Joaquin Valley into which he would blow mightily and then wad up carefully as if wrapping a dead bird.

A howl went off in a corner as Ruy Lopez, the bride's older brother, said something which set off an explosion of laughter. Ruy was drinking champagne without restraint, contributing to what would become a catastrophic hangover of unprecedented proportions. But that would be later. Much later. Now was now. Now there was rhythm and flow and laughter, affection, dancing and fun. Now he was happy. His baby sister, Esmeralda, had just married Judge Quintana and the wedding had been wonderful. Even the earthquake had added to the ceremony. "That wedding was earthshaking." Laughter. He looked around enjoying the response to his wit, as his short, chubby wife, Amapola, who was dark as cocoa, continued to perspire and worry about the food.

Ruy walked across the hall to chat with his mistress, Mrs. Birdwell, and her spectacular daughter, Alexis. He was surprised they had come. Alexis was so beautiful she was beyond fantasy. His affair with her mother was very polite, very proper, like a lemon cupcake or a small chef's salad with Thousand Island dressing on the side. When they made love she would always hush him as if he were in church, "Darling, shhhh." She liked to make love to the music of Guy Lombardo. Ruy looked at Alexis and was embarrassed, as much for the music as for the affair he was having with her mother. While making love, Winifred often called him by his full name: Ruiz Lopez Mondragon. But, most of the time it was "Roo-Eez," or "baby," a word she used awkwardly like a nonsmoker holding a cigarette. "Oh, Roo-Eez, bay-bee," she would say, "I'm climbing to the stars." Her husband had gone to Brazil on a business trip and had never returned. He had met an alluring twenty-one-year-old woman with cinnamon skin who smelled of apples and decided to stay. Can you blame him?

Ruy's affair with Mrs. Birdwell was so very discreet and cordial. Sometimes she would even wear woolen socks to keep her feet warm. Ruy did not quite understand the subtlety of the affair because Ruy did not quite understand subtlety. If you were happy you should declare it, sing it out. If you were sad you should cry. If you were hungry you should eat. If you wanted to get drunk you should drink booze. If you felt sensuous you should make love. A man reaching the peak of masculine sexuality should not have to cover his feelings like someone burping into a bouquet of pussy willows. No wonder Mr. Birdwell had split for Brazil. But then maybe that's the way all Anglos made love: silently, politely, listening to Guy Lombardo music, wearing woolen socks: guilty New England sex. Egg salad on white bread with mayonnaise once a week. Perhaps, though, it was best not to tinker with the relationship. Hers was the largest garden, and biggest account, on his entire gardening route. And, besides, an affair was an affair, another chapter in the book, another notch on the gun.

But, what the hell was she talking about now? "The wonder and power of matrimony: two souls united . . ." She sounded like Father *In*Clemente trying to pass for sober. "Don't you agree, Mr. Lopez?" He looked at Winifred's daughter. My God, she was staggering, beautiful and yet totally out of reach: man's greatest frustration, thought Ruy. She had caught the attempt at formality, distance, the "Mr. Lopez." He wondered if Alexis knew. Ruy smiled awkwardly. "Yes, yes, of course." He also wondered if his wife, Amapola, suspected anything.

The band erupted once again playing a mambo, adding to the sounds and sights and whirlpool of voices, commotion and people that jammed the Mission Dolores Parish Hall that night.

Quintana's old law partners were there, as were the judges, the state senators, the assembly aides, the city commissioners, dignitaries from the Central and South American

consulates. Two members of the San Francisco Board of Supervisors were there. Even the Mayor of the City and County of
San Francisco was there. And it wasn't even an election year.
The banker, Don Mario Castro, "The Prince of the Mission
District," was there along with his muscular daughter, Alicia,
who looked like a man; Terry Santamaría, the head of the
Mexican-American Joint Alliance (MAJA) made a brief appearance, as did Bunny García's good friend, Marisol, who
wore a costume that consisted mostly of veils.

"Dolores, do you see what Marisol is wearing?" asked
Señorita Lucrecia.

"Yes, dear, isn't it indecent," said Lucrecia. "You can
almost see her *cosa*."

"Disgusting."

"Indecent."

Marisol was a "Moorish gypsy" who owned the Marisol
Emporium of Psychic Counseling and Healing, where Bunny
García plied her trade.

Manny Caballos's daughter, Celine, was there with her
boyfriend, Bobby Bastón. She was flushed. For Celine, presenting Bobby was high commotion, high excitement. She
was with her Tito, her Robertito, her little Robert, and she
introduced him grandly, as if she were introducing the Bour-
bon King of Spain, Juan Carlos himself.

"Señora Lopez, I'd like you to meet Tito, a good friend of
mine . . ." she would gasp. She was so flustered her words
would tumble out in great disarray. The smug Tito, Robertito, little Robert, the object of Celine's awe, would smile
coyly, a bit smugly, a visiting dignitary, a prince from the
capital come to pay respect to the provinces. Perhaps he
should not have come. The only thing missing was a symbol,

a ring which the locals could kiss as they genuflected. Celine was practically dancing as she introduced her Tito, her Robertito, her little Robert, "I'd like you to meet Bobby Bastón," accent on the "o" in Bastón. God, how he hated to be called Bobby. That's what he was called as a boy. He had outgrown that. He had also outgrown Bastón. He now went by Báston, accent on the first syllable, which sounded more English, less Hispanic. After all . . . in this society, a lawyer had to . . .

Caballos glanced over at his daughter and smiled. There was approval, even tenderness in his glance. What a lovely prize his daughter would present some man. Bobby Bastón, with his law degree from Hastings, could be the one. She was, of course, much too good for him. He was too affected, too effete. He could pass for a gay. Besides, he had not proposed to her yet. What was the matter with him? Was there a brighter, more attractive jewel in the entire world? *¡Idiota!*

Señorita Lucrecia and Señorita Dolores—who together had logged nearly sixteen decades of virginity—were talking about, what else?, the pregnant Amalia Alegre. While across from them Delfina Varela was staring out at the stars, contemplating the terms of her pact with the Devil; absolutely convinced that the earthquake had been a sign of approval from the Devil. "I understand your needs, Delfina. I have a few other projects going. I will get back to you as soon as I can, sweetie, not to worry." That's the way devils talked, "sweetie."

Bunny García was talking to Judge Abelardo Quintana. "I also sell other things," she said, nudging the judge with her elbow. She threw her head back and laughed, revealing a golden canine tooth. Instinctively, her hand went up to cover the exposed tops of a pair of lovely brown breasts, which the judge kept admiring. So that Judge Abelardo Quintana would not misinterpret her meaning, Bunny winked and nudged him with her elbow and added, "Any time you want to party, Abe, just let me know." Bunny handed the judge a shiny maroon card. Printed on the card was Bunny's name and telephone number. Beneath her name were the words "Expert Psychic Counseling and Therapy." "Any time you need a little therapy just give me a little jingle," said Bunny laughing, covering the tops of her breasts once again. "If you know what I mean, Abe. *¿Sabes?*"

"*Sí. ¿Cómo no? Sí,*" said Quintana, his gaze returning appreciatively to the exposed tops of Bunny García's fine, brown breasts.

The judge, who had forgotten most of his Spanish, dearly loved to speak the language and used it as best he could. His children actually spoke better Spanish than he did. After all, they had learned Spanish at the universities from college professors not from farm workers or seamstresses. His daughters would often correct him.

"*Papi,* please. Don't say, '*asina.*' That's the way the rabble from East Los Angeles say, '*así.*' And the judge, who had grown up in East Los Angeles and who had learned his Spanish from his seamstress mother, would smile kindly at his children and apologize.

The commotion and din in the hall began to subside.

"*Órale, órale. Cht-cht-cht.*" Ruy Lopez was urging everyone to be silent. His father, his tearful, sloppily sentimental father, Mauricio, was about to propose a toast.

"I want to dedicate this toast to you, my daughter, Esmeralda. Or, as we used to call you when you were a little baby, '*Peditos.*' "

A titter could be heard, for *peditos* means "little farts" in Spanish. Esmeralda rolled her eyes hoping to die right there on the spot, at her own wedding. Raising a glass of champagne, her father continued.

"To you, Esmeralda, soul of my soul, seed of my loins, blood of my blood, tear of my tears, heart of my heart, does a simple, silly man dedicate this simple, silly toast. Torn from your mother's flesh, suckled at her breasts, you arrived to bring us hope, to bring us light, to bring us sunshine and joy, flowers and bread, wine, oil, grief and hope. For, from the bitter despair of our boring lives, did we clean up after you knowing that in the end . . ."

Ruy Lopez turned around; a sobbing could be heard behind him.

"*¡Mira!*"

"Look!"

"Over there."

"Pelon's beginning to cry."

The bald Pelon was having difficulty containing his sentimentality. Ruy rolled his eyes, walked over to him.

"Take it easy, Pelon," Ruy whispered, placing his hand on Pelon's shoulder.

"I'm sorry, *carnal*, I cannot help myself."

Pelon, the neighborhood's portrait photographer, would weep at baptisms and funerals, even at birthday parties and confirmations. He had wept earlier at the wedding ceremony, right after Delfina Varela had rebelled against Catholicism and before the earthquake. Pelon would cry at just about any occasion, for any reason. It all started when Pelon lost his beloved parrot, Pepe, which he had used as a prop to photograph children in his Mission District studio. The parrot, who could imitate the sounds of gunshots and sirens, was a neighborhood favorite. Pelon was so proud of Pepe that he would present small shows in his home which were attended by neighborhood children who would scream hysterically at the parrot's imitations. When Pepe died of food poisoning—he had eaten twelve jalapeño peppers one day in a fit of elation—Pelon went to pieces. After that, everything and everyone reminded him of his happy times with his beloved parrot. Now Pelon wept openly, without restraint or shame, at every occasion.

It would begin slowly, the crying. Great glossy tears would fill his eyes. A handkerchief would appear; a dab left, a dab right, a swipe at the nose, more tears, more hanky and then a deep sigh turning reluctantly into a whimper and then into a full sob and more tears. And before you could say Miguel de Cervantes Saavedra, there he was, this grown man, weeping out loud, in pieces, an absolute mess, crying at the Shortness and Sweetness of Life. As those around him would shake their heads and reach for their own handkerchiefs, Pelon would choke for air, swallowing, sobbing and honking like some high-flying bird. Others around him would take up his crying, especially the children, until everything would dissolve into a sloppy, sentimental mess. The only thing that would salvage the situation was laughter, especially when Pelon would blow his nose like some mighty trumpeting goose flying north to Canada to rejoin its flock.

The bride's father, who could see his toast turning into Pelon's sentimental feast, raised his glass, signaling an end to the toast as Pelon unleashed a final unstoppable torrent of tears, followed by another blast into his handkerchief.

The wet-faced Pelon forced a smile, exposing a row of terrible teeth. "I'm so happy," he said as he reached over menacingly to embrace Ruy Lopez. Ruy looked around and forced a grin, trapped in Pelon's predatorial embrace.

Shark Salazar and Los Falcones began a salsa tune that started out with a flourish on the timbales, flushing the dancers to the middle of the dance floor once again.

Pressing through the dancers was Ruy Lopez accompanied by Lourdes Pacheco, the pretty wife of Conde Pacheco, a petty racketeer whose city hall connections gave him the guise of respectability. She was tall, slender and wore a sheer purple and maroon dress that billowed when she turned. She was a shy woman and yet out on the dance floor she was transformed. Her movements were sure and flowing, and the men and women watching her nodded in approval at her poise and grace and beauty.

Up on the bandstand Shark Salazar pointed in the direction of Pelon, who was staring at Lourdes Pacheco with an open mouth ready to cry once again. No one enjoyed the attention being paid Lourdes Pacheco more than her own husband, Conde Pacheco. Although he hated to dance, he approved of his wife's gracefulness and beauty and, above all, the sight of other men ogling her. Conde Pacheco saw the look of yearning on Pelon's face and produced his famous grin.

Conde Pacheco's grin was excessive, the teeth too exposed, the mouth too wide. In photographs it always looked as if a United States Marine Corps bayonet had just been inserted up to the hilt into the back of his neck. The pink gums above two rows of white, even teeth: molars, incisors. The teeth first and then the theatrical moustache, and, guiding these, was a large, sharp nose. He would introduce himself with a "How DO you do?" and the forced, alarming grin would appear. "How DO you do?" he would ask, holding a hand a little too long, and women would pull away and adjust their dresses. "How DO you do?" and men would note the two-handed handshake, the grabbing palms, the moist hands and they would mentally check the location of their wallets.

In the center of the floor, Ruy Lopez was dancing, enjoying the sight of the dancers around him, the smiles. Hands touched, joined together and then separated. He was filled with joy. And liquor. He was out somewhere, away, turning in great, powerful loops, whirling dizzily through a swirl of dancers and laughter, and then out beyond that to the sea and the stars. Now he was surrounded by warmth, a diver swimming through formations of bright coral and kelp which occasionally reached out to touch him, and for several wonderful minutes he was powerful, invincible and immortal.

Lights were dimmed. A single set of beams created a silver shaft around the dancers. In Ruy's fantasy the dancers appeared as if in a maze, a glittering maze that slowly turned around him and Lourdes as the dancers moved in unison to the beat of the music. It was Ruy's perfect shimmering night of sounds and colors and laughter and aromas of food and perfume and liquor and smoke.

When the dance ended, Ruy escorted Lourdes back to a grinning Conde Pacheco. *"Órale, mano,"* said Conde Pacheco. "Beautiful wedding."

*"Epa,* thanks, *mano."*

Someone bumped into Ruy. He turned to see Delfina Varela. "Excuse me," said Delfina.

"Ruy, have you met Delfina?" asked Conde Pacheco. "Ruy, this is my aunt, Delfina Varela."

"How are you?"

Delfina looked away. She felt embarrassed. She had been

thinking about the Devil. Too shy to look at Ruy directly, Delfina offered her hand, looked at her shoes and said, "How do you do? Any friend of Conde is not my friend."

"What?"

"She's kidding. You know."

"I am not kidding," said Delfina Varela. "Everyone knows that Conde is a *ratón*. He once sold me a watch that was stolen and a TV that blew up."

"You'll have to excuse Tía Delfina. She's a little, you know . . ." Conde circled a finger by his temple. "*¿Sabes?* Tía Delfina keeps talking about a Cadillac. Says the earthquake was a sign that she'll get one."

"You think you are so funny, Conde. Just wait. When I get my car you and your *ratero* friends will be jealous."

"I better get back, Conde," said Ruy.

"*Vale,*" said Conde.

"*Vale.*"

Someone screamed.

Everyone turned to see a phenomenon: Ombligo the Fat was approaching the dance floor.

Five-five, three twenty-five. Ombligo's fatness went beyond the corporeal. He embodied the spirituality of the spherical, the splendor of it, of round things that convey power and presence: a sun, a moon, a great mammal or a powerful bureaucrat, which he was.

He moved ominously, a silent liner moving carefully into a Caribbean harbor filled with expensive yachts. There was a feeling there of restrained danger: a circus elephant moving slowly past bleachers filled with birthday-party children. One dared not think of stopping or hindering that inertia: the liner would end up slicing through several wharf warehouses, spilling coffee beans and Toyotas into the harbor; the elephant could topple tent poles and bleachers bringing Teresita's festive birthday party to a quick, unfortunate and unforgettable conclusion.

When Ombligo walked out on the dance floor some reached across small tables to tap an arm; others brought hand up to mouth to suppress a smile. A buzz arose, a bit of smiling, a giggle, an anticipation of silliness and clumsiness. Until Ombligo began to dance. Then and only then did the commotion subside. The scoffers realized the extent of their skepticism as mouths gaped open in disbelief.

"My God." The phrase was repeated. *"Dios mío."* Some began clapping, for Ombligo danced well, very well indeed, with his partner and girl friend, the pretty Veronica.

*"Mi gordito,"* said Veronica, a term she used with infinite sweetness, as he took her in his small hands with their thick, stubby fingers, and stepped forward, his small, round foot introducing a mambo and a shaft of silver light from a ceiling spotlight. The great mammal had entered the water delicately and was about to swim expertly in the weightlessness of music.

Now Bunny García wanted to dance. She was being as subtle as the earthquake which had struck earlier. She went over to Ruy and began shifting from foot to foot in time to the music. She looked at him and smiled. Her thick lips were bursting with lipstick: crimson red and glistening. Ruy smiled back. He followed the redness of her lips and she gave him a slight nod of the head, a small hook of the shoulder and a shake of the fanny, and he found himself following her out to the dance floor.

*¡Hijo!* She was a good dancer, and he had been drinking

enough not to care now about anything or anyone anymore. The air in the hall was hot. Whenever Bunny got close to him he could smell her overpowering cologne fighting a losing battle against her body odors. She was smooth, and very sexy. She smiled and her gold tooth suddenly flashed like a warning in the silvery light. They would break away easily and then glide back toward each other. He reached for her and she responded and they went out and then came back together again. It was all very smooth, very easy. Ruy enjoyed it all so very, very much. Ombligo and Veronica swam by him and touched him as if from a dream or distant memory. All that seemed to matter now was this place and this perfect moment of dancing and the music of Los Falcones.

And then . . .

And then it happened . . .

In the middle of this dream and Ruy's pleasant tipsiness on a warm evening, all of the lights went out, not just in the hall but everywhere. Girls began screaming, and then there was silence and darkness.

The stars appeared clean and shiny at the windows in a moonless night. For a few seconds no one spoke as somewhere a powerful motor came to a halt with a tired, groaning wheeze. Ruy, by now rather tipsy and dizzy from dancing with Bunny García, found himself turning in circles, spinning through the darkness.

And then from somewhere, from a dream or remembrance or longing, there came the smell of vanilla as a sensuous mouth pressed against his, a tongue sought out his lips in an incredible kiss. In the darkness, he was holding someone in his arms, a slim waist, and he could feel her hair at his eyes. He was surrounded by the smell of vanilla and suddenly he was swaying, surrendering, falling through space. Her hair was in his face, brushing against his eyes. Her breasts pressed against his chest. And he and she were touching and embracing totally and kissing passionately in that almost absolute darkness. Now he was floating out, out toward the sea, and she was giving him everything in that dream, and he released her.

*"Mi hombre hermoso,"* she whispered and through the stars and distant sounds she pulled away from him and was gone. My beautiful man, she had called him, and he knew he had to follow that voice, that slender waist, that fragrance of vanilla. Ruy, by now entangled in his own dream, knew he had to follow. He pursued her, tried to follow, he wanted to embrace that slender waist once again, only to find himself stumbling forward uncontrollably. A shoulder, an arm.

Matches were being struck now. The sparks of cigarette lighters flashed into flame. The buzz in the hall increased. In his frenzy Ruy had grabbed the bald-headed Pelon. In the bubbling, flickering lights, Ruy looked around desperately for his spectacular phantom.

There was no one. She had vanished. There was only Pelon looking at him sadly. Where was she? On the left was his wife, Amapola, who smelled of coriander. On the other side was Bunny García, who smelled of cheap toilet water and decayed cabbage leaves. She was still swaying from the dance.

Who was she? Where was she? Where had she gone?

Ruy became frantic, a fish swimming through darkness, the crowd, the sputtering light, as he searched for that slim waist, that aroma. For several seconds she had given him everything and then had disappeared, and she had called him, *"Mi hombre hermoso,"* my beautiful man. What madness. Had it all been a dream, an imagining, a fantasy, a figment of his own fertile imagination? Things like that happened only in movies. Ruy was puzzled, excited. Who was she?

There next to him was Pelon, embarrassed, presenting him a forlorn smile. My God, what terrible teeth. This wasn't the stuff of fantasy.

But, wait, maybe it had been Pelon? Could that kindly gentleman, the one with the hair-trigger tears, could he have lusted after Ruy all these years? Perhaps Pelon, unable to restrain himself any longer, had been responsible for the power outage. Perhaps he had carefully planned the entire thing: arranged with someone to have all the lights turned out at just the right moment when, closest to Ruy, there in the darkness, he could consummate his yearning, his desperate, illicit lust? The thought was revolting to Ruy. Ruy glared at Pelon who, as usual, looked embarrassed. Disgusting man, thought Ruy. Such an elaborate ploy for one hot kiss. Ruy felt like spitting. The thought made him want to punch poor Pelon's smiling face. It was revolting to think about it, but then who could know? It happened. Life was strange. Nowadays men dressed like women and women dressed like men and scientists were making babies in bottles and creating mice in the laboratory.

Pelon smiled at Ruy. "The lights must have gone out," Pelon rasped.

Good Lord, thought Ruy, any imbecile could figure that out. He didn't have to be told. Ruy felt like slapping Pelon's face.

But, wait a minute. Wait a minute. It couldn't have been Pelon. He always reeked of those cheap cigars he loved to smoke, the ones that stained his teeth. And his waist was anything but slim. Besides, his voice was low and gravelly, not the angelic voice that had whispered those immortal words, *"Mi hombre hermoso."* And, oh, for Heaven's sake, why hadn't he thought about that? How silly. Ruy struck his forehead with the palm of his hand. How could he possibly have gotten entangled in Pelon's aromatic hair? Pelon was completely bald.

Ruy, embarrassed by his own terrible suspicions, reached over and embraced Pelon. "I'm sorry, Pelon. It could not have been you."

Pelon, who had always felt the world was populated by lunatics, said, "At's all right. Don' worry," and offered up yet another sad smile before this particular lunatic could do something rash. To clear his emotional palate, Pelon started to sniffle.

Who was she? Ruy glanced around quickly. By the light of the sputtering matches and cigarette lighters Ruy could make out Amalia Alegre who appeared ready to give birth at any minute. She was perspiring uncontrollably. Not her. Too much sweat. Too pregnant. He could hardly reach around her. Ruy moved through the hall in a daze of tiredness and sensuality and opened a door into the starry night where he felt the air cool on his face.

Outside, couples were talking and laughing.

"This wedding had everything."

Some were embracing. Ruy could make out the silhouette of a standing couple pressed together in the midst of a deep kiss, and he could feel his own beating desire, a desire neither wife nor mistress could appease.

*"Mi hombre hermoso,"* she had called him. My beautiful man.

# Ruy Lopez

"*Mi hombre hermoso*," she had whispered to him. "My beautiful man."

# 4. A Hangover of Catastrophic Proportions

Ruy reentered the hall where, by the flickering light of matches and candles, Amalia Alegre was writhing on the floor.

A scream went up and a crowd formed a ring. How strange, thought Ruy, how primitive: people gathering in a torchlit circle. In his continuing dream, Ruy approached the crowd.

Amalia, the ever-fertile Amalia Alegre, was giving birth.

"*¡Qué bárbaro!*" said the gossip Señorita Dolores. "How disgusting!"

"Indecent," said Señorita Lucrecia. "See. I told you. These hussies will do anything for attention."

"Silly cow," said Señorita Dolores. "Why does everything have to be so public? Even cattle do it in barns. Why can't these people do this in the privacy of their own houses?"

"They would miss the attention," said Señorita Lucrecia. "And just think, no one even knows who the father is."

"Isn't that just terrible?"

"It is awful."

"Shhhh."

Girls could be heard giggling.

The pink Amalia glowed with fertility. She smiled painfully, looking profoundly embarrassed as she began the miracle of birth. Right there. On the floor of the Mission Dolores Parish Hall by the light of matches and lighters.

A tiny black head of hair appeared, followed by gray shoulders and arms and then a twisting, appalling umbilical cord.

In Ruy's starlit ocean appeared a small whitecap of nausea.

It was Pelon who saw it first. "It's a woman," he said as he began to cry.

Bunny García screamed, "It's a little baby female."

For all the world, the bastard child looked like someone very familiar. It was Pelon, through his tears, who said what everyone was thinking.

"She looks like Judge Abelardo Quintana. Look, if you put glasses on her and give her an Adolf Hitler moustache . . ."

"*¡Cállate!*" said Bunny García. "Shut up!" When she turned to see that Pelon was crying she offered him a handkerchief that smelled of toilet water.

Ruy staggered away, suddenly feeling seasick by the awful scene of birth. The site of the spiraling umbilical cord emerging from a miniature version of his new brother-in-law, the Honorable Judge Abelardo Quintana, was more than he could bear.

Ruy wandered out of the hall. Somewhere, from a distant memory, his wife Amapola was calling him, asking him where he was going.

"Out."

He walked away from the swaying hall, through a neighborhood cast in darkness, past a cat eating a mouse, past a tilting house where, in a room lit by candles, a naked woman standing at a window was singing, "You Are My Sunshine."

A dog had tipped over a metal container and was pawing through garbage. Ruy went over to pet the dog as it growled and exposed a row of teeth.

Lights. Traffic. A blaring horn. A bus. A bed. And sleep.

He found himself in bed, clothes and all, perspiring. He hoped, sincerely hoped, it was his own bed in his own home.

*"Mi hombre hermoso,"* she had whispered as he drifted out to a tossing, restless sea.


Delfina Varela was certain the power outage had been the work of the Devil. After all, Father *In*Clemente always referred to him as the Prince of Darkness. The very name made Delfina quiver. Another thing that convinced her that the outage was the work of the Devil was the fact that, in the confusion, a hand had rubbed her bottom. It had shocked her. Only later did she admit to herself that she had actually enjoyed having a strange hand rub her bottom in the dark, just like in the old days with her husband, Panchito, before he died of cirrhosis of the liver. Perhaps it was best that she never learned that the bottom rubber had been the ring bearer, Eufemio Galian, who had been looking for a light switch. When her bottom was rubbed all Delfina could think of was, "Is it you, Devil? Have you come to tempt me and to claim my immortal soul?" Needless to say Delfina was disappointed when the lights were turned back on before the Devil could ravish her or even tempt her for keeps.

.  .  .

For Ruy the night was filled with turmoil: bubbling gases and gurgling deep, primeval fears and perspiration and much tossing and great sorrowful wheezing turns which wrapped all of the covers around his left leg. When Amapola arrived and got into bed, it was like trying to sleep next to a mighty wounded beast or a small natural disaster.

Ruy had overindulged.

He would mumble, try to sleep on his stomach, turn on his side and then flip over quickly onto his back. He was crawling through the night grabbing at his pillow, pushing it to the mattress; a half nelson became a bear hug. He sought a handle here, a crevice there, anything to hang on to as he fell through the night in looping, gliding circles. There was no graceful dancing now; no feelings of invincibility and immortality; only survival. He was grabbing at everything: the sweat-soaked pillow, blankets, sheets, even Amapola, trying to break his fall.

"Hey, wait a minute," yelled Amapola.

"*Aiii, Diosito, Diosito mío,*" Ruy groaned.

He found himself walking through the house, the floor cold against his hot feet, as the clock quickly counted off the seconds of his mortal life, ridiculing his intemperance.

"Ticktock, ticktock, tsk-tsk, tsk-tsk."

Ruy lifted the edge of his lip, "Shut up."

"*Aiii, Diosito, Diosito mío.*" Ruy begged God for forgiveness for every sin, every indiscretion he had ever committed in his entire lifetime.

And then the headache. It began as a sweet baby's gurgle and turned into a poignant train whistle heard somewhere off in memory, out in the distance, reminding him of faraway places and gay, nostalgic, happy times forever gone. But then the train's sound got closer and the crossing gates went down across his eyes and before he knew it the engine began to roar in his ears as the entire Midnight Express was crashing through his head: gondola cars sloshing swill, flatcars bearing military hardware and cement trucks, boxcars filled with ball bearings and sewer pipe and then a thousand smelly passenger cars filled with blaspheming, battle-dressed soldiers all belching and lusting for sex.

"*¡Pendejo!*" yelled a gold-toothed Mexican conductor as the train flushed by.

Ruy groaned, "Holy Mother of God."

On this warm night of Ruy's anguish two fat lovers, Judge Abelardo Quintana and Esmeralda, bathed nude in the cool waters of San Gregorio Beach located south of San Francisco on Highway 1. They had stopped there on their way to their honeymoon site in Monterey. They would sit on the sand and, in the moonless night, gaze out at the dark sea from the edge of the continent and then up to the bright starry wonder of what was, at least for them, a perfect, memorable night.

"My dear, sweet Esmeralda," whispered Judge Quintana to his nineteen-year-old bride, stroking her breast. "What would I do without you, *querida?*" That night they made love fiercely, Esmeralda giggling and squealing like a sow, and for one hour they became beautiful fat, dark gods gamboling across warm, golden fields, for God has given fat people the ability to make love sublimely.

Toward morning a bird alighted on the branches of the sycamore tree in Ruy's back yard. The tree was located outside the open windows of the bedroom. The bird was angry at Ruy and was screaming at him in a variety of voices and chirps and languages. Ruy was convinced. The bird was scolding and ridiculing him.

The bird sang out:

"You are a *pendejo* of the first waters. I simply cannot believe how stupid you are. You are fat. You are ignorant. You are gullible. I can't stand your fatness, your incurable excess, your stupidity and violence. I cannot stand your vanity and cupidity," chirped the bird. "Take that for your laziness, and this for your emotionalism and sentimentality. And that for your wastefulness and profligate spending. Take that and that and then that again, you scum, you snake, you rat," said the little bird who happened to be a mockingbird.

*"Aii, Diosito mío."* Ruy, in his misery, covered his ears with his pillow. Even the little birds found him disgusting.

# 5. Delfina's Pact with the Devil

The fortune cookie message read, "The best way to overcome temptation is to succumb to it." Delfina had to look up the word "succumb" to find out what it meant.

"*Ah, vaya,* it means to give in, Benjie," she said, addressing her overweight cat who kept meowing for his dinner. "I'm sorry, my baby, you must be so hungry. I went to *El Chino* Fong and got you some nice shrimp in bean curd sauce, the kind you like, *precioso.*"

When Benjie had been fed she returned to the fortune cookie message, which she found very troubling for temptation was something that Delfina had been contemplating for a very long time.

Delfina Varela, who went to church religiously, had been praying to God for years for a major temptation. Delfina felt so strong religiously that she knew she could overcome any kind of temptation. She wanted to be tested like a saint. Well, that's where it started; where it ended was at a totally different bus depot. Funny where things sometimes begin and where the hell they end up.

She knew she could resist temptation. After all, she recited a full rosary every day. In her living room, next to the framed picture of President John F. Kennedy, was a picture of the Sacred Heart of Jesus, a handsome young man with long blond hair looking up mournfully, his bleeding forehead bearing a crown of thorns. In his right hand he held a bleeding heart ringed with thorns and pierced with a cross. Delfina wondered why anyone would want to hold a messy thing like that in his hand. Both the picture of John F. Kennedy and the one of the Sacred Heart of Jesus had been blessed with the holy water by Father *In*Clemente.

Something else that has to be considered in looking for a motive was the votive; the fact that Delfina lit two votive candles in church every Sunday. At two dollars apiece that wasn't peanuts. Four dollars a week for two votive candles had to be budgeted by Delfina. Were she to keep accurate or even passable bookkeeping records this would probably have been entered under a column titled, "Sacrifices" or "Sufferings." With all of this spiritual fire insurance, Delfina knew she could resist temptation. So she wanted to be subjected to one. Honestly, the things that got into that woman's mind. After all, went her logic, she wasn't getting any younger and just once in her life, before she died, she wanted to experience a strong temptation.

The trouble was that, year after year, temptation never came. Oh, to be sure, there was always the little stuff. There was always the temptation to call Father *In*Clemente a *pendejo.* But she could never do that to his face even though everyone knew he was one. If she did she would only have to reveal that in Confession. And the chances were *igual Pascual,* even Steven, that the Confessor listening to her reveal her sins would be none other than—who else?—that *gran pendejo,* Father *In*Clemente. No, she couldn't do that. There was also the great temptation to say something impolite to Señorita Lucrecia and Señorita Dolores. But if she succumbed to nastiness she would only be stooping to their level and add to the list of things they could prattle about.

No, what Delfina Varela sought was Major Temptation, the kind that tempted saints. "Delfina, eat ye of this Fuji apple and you will know everlasting glory and good sex. Here, Delfina, take ye and eat of this." That kind of temptation. Delfina's hopes for a Major Temptation grew stronger, her spiritual longing more intense. But her prayers went unanswered. She began praying not so much for the salvation of her immortal soul anymore—*ya que,* that was getting to be old hat—so much as for the appearance of a Major Temptation. When temptation failed to appear, Delfina prayed even harder until, for some unfathomable reason, she began to pray directly to the Devil himself, *El Diablo,* the Prince of Darkness.

It was when her bad feet really began to bother her that she seriously began to think about a car.

"Bunions," said Dr. Figueroa as if condemning her to purgatory for the rest of her life, which indeed he had.

"*¿Qué?* What is that?"

"*Juanetes.*"

"Ah, *vaya, juanetes.*"

She had once seen a movie on TV with James Cagney and Pat O'Brien where the doctor tells the little boy's father, following an accident, "This child will never be able to walk again for as long as he lives," as the mother begins to wail. Dr. Figueroa's pronouncement was no less shocking.

It was shortly after that that her sister, Chencha, broke her hip. The trip to Fresno to see her ailing sister had been terrible, extremely time-consuming and painful. It was that trip that finally convinced Delfina that she *had* to have a car. She had walked from her home to a Mission District bus stop; waited for a bus next to a youth playing a ghetto blaster and taken the graffiti-marked bus to the Trans-Bay Terminal in downtown San Francisco. At the terminal she boarded another bus that had taken her across the Bay to the Oakland train station. From there she had traveled by train to Fresno, where she had boarded a Fresno bus and then transferred to another rural bus before arriving at her sister's house exhausted.

"If we had a car," she told her beloved cat, "we could go see Chencha more often." Benjie agreed.

Delfina began to link her need for Temptation with her need for Wheels, and then, when her bunions began to *really* bother her, she concentrated on the Wheels.

Well, as with the beginning of most wars, one stupid thing just seems to lead to another until the whole damn thing just simply gets out of control and there you are one day, looking up from your bunker near the Reichstag, your national capital looking like the Chicago Fire.

And there too was Delfina Varela that day at the spectacularly garish wedding of Judge Abelardo Quintana and Esmeralda Lopez—when all of a sudden all of the spiritual circuits in Delfina's head misfired and reversed their spiritual polarity.

# Manny Caballos

His impossible dream of meaningful Hispanic political
activism could not be extinguished.

# 6. MAJA

"*Pendejos*," screamed Manny Caballos. "*Brutos.*" What was taking place was a regular meeting of the volunteer political association known as MAJA, the Mexican-American Joint Alliance. The monthly MAJA meetings were held on the first Tuesday of every month at the Club Ba-Ba-Lu, an abandoned dance hall owned by Manny Caballos that was located on Mission and Twenty-second streets. No one really knew why the organization was a "joint" one nor what constituted the alliance; the important thing was that the name produced a nice acronym.

These meetings are silly, time-consuming and frustrating, thought Caballos, a former MAJA president who had become disillusioned with the group's apathy. His own daughter Celine would run circles around these *pendejos* who were always wanting to borrow the Ba-Ba-Lu for their group functions, or money-losing dances. These same individuals were always asking him for "a little donation"—a contribution "for the Blessed Mother," "for Holy Mother Church," or worst of all *"Para la Causa,"* for "the Cause," whatever that meant. He was a sucker for Hispanic causes and political candidates and they knew it. What was the Cause? Their own self-interests? The Cause invariably was tied to some direct personal gain for the individual with the Cause. Just because he had the sense to run a profitable business they would ask him for money as if he owed it to them; money for the dance, money for the candidate, for the school board, money for the Sisters of Mercy, for the dance troupe, for the area museum. My God, it never stopped. They reminded him of Chancho, his cat. Whenever Chancho saw him entering the back yard, the cat would always lick his chops, ready to be fed.

Caballos looked across the room. Sitting there adjusting a microphone was Benny Velasquez from Channel 14—one of the Spanish-language channels in the San Francisco Bay Area which specialized in local news and Mexican soap operas. Who could get that channel anyway? Crews from Channel 14 were always showing up with their bright lights and secondhand equipment and anxious reporters who poked microphones into people's mouths and then asked the silliest questions. The cameramen were invariably bored San Francisco Chinese who didn't speak a word of Spanish and who always kept looking at their watches and at the doors and windows.

As for the so-called Hispanic leaders: There was Sergio Barajas, Barajas the Clown, running for Mayor of the City and County of San Francisco. There was also Chacon Belmonte running for supervisor, doing everything he possibly could to get himself defeated. Now he was running around with somebody else's wife, while his own wife was pregnant. You'd think he had just discovered nooky. Caballos looked across the hall at Oscar de la Peña, who had run for mayor in the last election. His campaign had been a fiasco, nothing less. A highly publicized hit-and-run traffic accident had gotten him the kind of campaign publicity de la Peña did not need. He had placed sixteenth in a field of eighteen, just ahead of a man who dressed in a clown costume who advocated free ice cream for all of the children of San Francisco, and behind a person listed as Divine Dina the Bubble Lady who spoke of salvation through soap bubbles. Who could take de la Peña seriously? He wanted to create a separate, independent state of Hispanics in the U.S. That sounded splendid. But who would run this new state, Oscar? You? Divine Dina the Bubble Lady?

Sometimes the articulate and impassioned Terry Santamaría had his moments. Santamaría was a particularly effective speaker. He was very good with reporters and looked nice on television. But, beyond a pat speech regarding the emergence of the U.S. Hispanic—a speech he had been giving for the past twenty years—there was nothing there. Santamaría had no burning vision, no sense of hope for himself or for Hispanics. Caballos hated to admit it: beyond his pat speech, Terry Santamaría was a dry well. And organizationally, Santamaría was a disaster. God, thought Caballos, his own Celine could teach Santamaría a thing or two. Although Terry was a genuine, gentle heart and meant well, he couldn't organize his own shoelaces. The Alliance meetings he chaired were fiascoes, meetings so totally disorganized and disoriented that members, out of sheer frustration and disgust, began shouting just to be heard. More than one of Santamaría's meetings had ended in fights.

Caballos fondly recalled the time Beltram Sotomayor had called Shorty Alarcon a *maricón,* a fairy. Naturally, Shorty had to attack Beltram in order to prove his *machismo.* It had been such a spectacle. A point of honor, just like the rumbles with the punk gangs he had grown up with in East Los Angeles.

And then there was the time the hotheaded Carmen Delgado had called Pilar Anaya a "Ged-demn-Puerto-Rican-*puta.*" Pilar, like a thrown knife, had rushed to scratch out Carmen's eyes only to be separated by the quick-thinking Pepe Maestro, who had managed to defray Pilar's rage by

grabbing her and squeezing one of her breasts. "Hey, mother-
fucker, stop that," Pilar had screamed, as the others yelled at
Pepe to either squeeze both breasts or to let the two go at each
other's throats. Theirs had been a long-standing animosity
and what better time to let them settle it than right there and
then in the middle of a MAJA meeting.

"Point of order," Santamaría had demanded. There had
followed much name-calling and stalking, much whining, but
very little contact—to everyone's disappointment—two midnight cats whining in the dark, posturing, screeching, reluc-
tant to strike. All of these encounters usually ended in a matter of minutes. But, they created indelible grudges which
were never forgotten or forgiven; hatreds that were passed on
to children and grandchildren. Boy-oh-boy, thought Señor
Caballos, sometimes it was tough being a Mexican.

But month after month, Caballos would return to these
painful gatherings. His impossible dream of meaningful Hispanic political activism could not be extinguished, even
though these meetings had a way of invariably turning into
frustration and nonsense. All MAJA members seemed to do
was berate "the System," whatever that meant. After a meeting of the Alliance, MAJA members would meet at the Blackthorn, a cheap neighborhood bar on Mission Street that had
passed from its original Irish owner to an Italian and then a
Mexican. The Mexican, in turn, had sold the bar to a woman
from Guatemala, who now ran it. The succession of owners
had paralleled the ethnic evolution of the entire Mission District. At the Blackthorn, MAJA members would talk about
power and, over stiff drinks, they would shout about the day,
the inevitable day of Hispanic political, economic and social
ascendancy. And, after too many drinks, they would be pie-

eyed and begin appointing each other to the offices of Secretary of State or Attorney General or Governor of the State of California. But the following day they would return to their law offices in *La Michon* where they could hardly keep decent secretaries because of the low wages they paid; and in the morning it would all be weak coffee and stale donuts, humiliating pursuits and outworn promises. They would listen to tired people describing failed lives, divorces, family altercations, or serve as court-appointed lawyers in traffic, petty theft and dope-arrest cases. That's what Hispanic Power amounted to in the Mission District of San Francisco.

At their annual nationwide MAJA political meetings, they would talk of dignity and patriotism, of political power and everlasting glory. Their speeches would be titled, "The Revolution," or "The Emergence of the Latino in the United States," headlines taken directly from the press, articles that appeared in major national publications: the *New York Times,* the *Washington Post,* the *Christian Science Monitor, Time* magazine, *Newsweek.* All of the television networks had mentioned It. All had done major pieces on It: the emergence and approaching political influence of U.S. Hispanics. The television programs were invariably titled, "The Awakening of the Sleeping Giant" or "The Inevitability of the Latino." All invariably cited the overwhelming numbers, the percentages. They would talk of the predominance of Hispanics in the United States, who, with their profound fertility, would someday outnumber blacks as the leading minority. The "leaders" of groups like MAJA, as well as of numerous other Hispanic organizations, all read these articles or saw the television presentations and they knew that, with their stale, tired disorganized "organizations," they were considered to be at the forefront of the Movement. The delusion/illusion went full circle. The media would point out the Hispanic political dream by quoting statistics and the words of Hispanic "leaders" or "spokespersons." These "leaders" in turn would see the articles and television programs and believe them and reinforce their own delusions.

Caballos surveyed the room as he felt the torn plastic on the chair he was sitting in. He wondered how many people had passed through the Ba-Ba-Lu. The place smelled of rancid food, body odors, stale cigarettes and urine. Had there ever been hope here; individuals coming here to relieve their loneliness? How many couples had met here? How many had danced together here amidst the garishness and the paper palm trees and beneath the mirrored glass ball that once sprayed dancers with its flashing, reflected light? How many had kissed for the very first time and then fallen in love, here amidst the loud colors and the tacky red vinyl booths that now always felt greasy?

Caballos wondered. He looked around. The Ba-Ba-Lu was now where, once a month, members of MAJA could reign supreme and strut like peacocks; here was where they could discuss issues of great political consequence. They would charge their own impoverished members fifty dollars a ticket to social events and then wonder why the turnouts were poor. At fund raisers they would invite prominent national figures who never accepted their invitations but whose public relations staffs would respond with letters that gushed of support for the "Hispanic Cause" so that once every two or four years their candidates could be photographed with Hispanic "leaders." These were invariably lily-white *gabacho* political candidates who came down to the Mission District to be filmed or videotaped eating a taco or wearing a sombrero proclaiming their loyalty to the "wonderfully varied multicultural richness of this city." And when these same politicians got elected to office, they would appoint a Hispanic sycophant to a meaningless but visible post. The politician would bring "his" Hispanic along to neighborhood meetings and point to him or her as an example of a "commitment to all of the people that make up this rich ethnic heritage of the City and County of San Francisco."

Caballos looked across the room and caught the eye of Victor Lopez, who headed the Mexican-American Judicial Fund and Educational Affiliation. Caballos shook his head; Victor smiled. The Affiliation, which Victor himself had founded, was a corporate-backed fund aimed at legally advocating the gerrymandering of California political districts by race. It was one of the few groups that were bringing about true, effective change that benefited Hispanics. Victor exploited his organization well. On the walls of his law office were photographs, in color, of Victor Lopez at a podium introducing the Governor of California. In another photograph, he smiled as he shook hands with the Vice President of the United States. A third saw him sitting at the same table with the Mayor of San Francisco.

Someone yelled out. All Caballos could hear was someone else's reply, ". . . Mexican Power!" Caballos winced. Power. These people, his people, spoke of power so naively. As if it could be bought by the pound. Let them talk emptily of power. Let them talk of the number of Hispanics in the United States, let them talk of influence and hope and political emergence. But as far as he, Caballos, was concerned, the only source of power was money. True power, true influence was right here in his breast pocket: in his checkbook. Money. That was the absolute source of power. Campaign contributions, substantial ones, could outyell these *pendejos* any day.

These then are the Hispanic leaders of our great and glorious tomorrow, thought Caballos, the ones who would foster the Great Hispanic Revolution in the United States. Perhaps Celine was right. Why bother? It all seemed so futile. Better to be led by clever children than by these nincompoops. But, what the hell, he thought. What does it all matter anyway? In the end what did it all come down to? These leaders would probably be no worse than the present pack of politicians now running the country who were always either bankrupting the country or declaring war. Except for a few rare moments, life seemed so silly, so very silly indeed.

His own daughter, Celine, would embarrass these "leaders" with her cleverness and business sense. But she disliked politics intensely and that was too bad. She had no political ambitions and had very early on assessed and rejected Hispanic political "activism" for what it really was: silly, frustrating, thankless.

A look of contentment appeared on Caballos's face, a pleasant thought. Manny Caballos's business was solid thanks to Celine. He had distribution routes all around the San Francisco Bay Area. To Bay Area bars and restaurants, he distributed Tehuacan and Peñafiel carbonated water from Mexico as well as rum, Mexican cognac and Mexican beer: Tecate, Dos Equis, Carta Blanca, Bohemia and that awful Corona, that donkey piss the yuppy *gringos* adored. He also distributed *masa* —the prepared dough for making tortillas—cactus and chili salsas and corn husks for making tamales as well as the Mexican sausage, chorizo, and other food and condiments. He owned two warehouses, one in South San Francisco ("South City") and the main one here in the Mission District. As for the Ba-Ba-Lu, he had purchased it as a favor to a friend who was going broke, and now Caballos was stuck with it; it stood as another monument to his sentimentality and benevolence.

In his business, Caballos employed his son, Carlos, a husky, vigorous brute who could pick up cases of beer with one hand. And in the back of his large, well-lit Mission District warehouse, a warehouse whose floors were waxed once a month, was an office, a back office away from the blare and brightness of the Mission District, an office he had paneled and redecorated, an office with solid, oak furniture and new computers. In that office sat Caballos's prize, his beauty, his most precious possession: Celine, his small, beautiful, fragrant daughter who always smelled of lemons and oranges. She possessed something his brutish son did not, something Caballos considered a gift from God the Father Almighty: a fine analytical mind and—may Heaven be blessed—a degree in accounting from Golden Gate University.

Let Carlos do the manual labor, let him lift crates and tote boxes, after all, oxen and elephants were needed to move logs and heavy loads—but let his small, dainty Celine wave her delicate fingers over his accounts like a magician producing rabbits and pigeons and tax write-offs. Accounts receivable, accounts payable, ledger entries, amortizations, capital expenditures: mysterious words which Manny Caballos could hardly understand, mysterious wires on a path which could trip up an entire business if one was careless. It was all so baffling to him, almost magical, but to his Celine these things were the very marrow of good enterprise. She was a true magician. She, with her scalpel entries which, in her delicate handwriting, produced power, true power: double-entry bookkeeping, amortizations, depreciations, tax write-offs. Lovely words which were a mystery to Manny Caballos, but which he knew meant the difference between a careful, easy business and endless nights of overbearing labor, between a truly wonderful vacation in Tahiti or another trip to Disneyland in Anaheim. She had modernized his entire operation, installed a communication system on the trucks and an inventory system which really worked. She had computerized everything. Now she was even talking about purchasing a third warehouse. "You really need one, *Papi,*" she said. "And it's not as if you can't afford one. Besides, San Francisco property is a good investment." Caballos frowned. If anyone but Celine or Carlos dared call him *"Papi"* he would break their legs. "And you really should get rid of the Ba-Ba-Lu. It just sits there as you pay taxes on it. Sell it for something, anything, and then invest the money."

"I will. But not now."

Caballos knew that his daughter was absolutely right. He had to get rid of the Ba-Ba-Lu and he would. Caballos smiled again. His thoughts were on Celine. Celine the magician. Celine the musician. Celine the angel. Thanks to her it all worked. Thanks to his lovely, beautiful daughter who, with her dainty fingers, could weave glorious works of art, similar to the fine drawings and paintings she had produced that now decorated his home and office. She was a skilled artist. It was magic, nothing less. Business had never been so good. Yes, the business was successful thanks to his happy, affectionate, stupid Carlos with his big hands and feet and his brute strength, and his beloved wispish Celine with her clever mind and delicate features. All worked effectively to insure the success and strength of Caballos and Son. For Christmas, what the hell, he would rename the company, change the name to "Caballos and Son and Daughter." Why not? Celine would be embarrassed. She would also point out the cost of having to order new stationery, envelopes, forms with the new name, signs for the building and trucks. But in the end she would hug him and kiss him and thank him appreciatively. And, most importantly, she would be totally sincere about it. And that's all that really mattered to him at his age. What the hell, it was his company, he could do with it what he wanted. After all, she was as responsible as anyone for their success, his new prosperity. She was more important to him than Carlos. If he didn't like it he could go straight to hell, get the hell out. He'd hire some other laborer. Caballos paused. No. He wouldn't. Carlos was his only son: a good boy, honest and loyal. And probably too dumb to get another job.

Caballos's thoughts returned to the MAJA meeting and then to a favorite fantasy. The thought warmed him. Perhaps someday there could be a Mexican in the White House. Think of it, a Mexican-American President of the United States of America. Someone like that guy up in Canada, what's his name, that Frenchie who had been Prime Minister and who could stand up and give perfect, beautiful speeches in both English and French. Only here it would be a Mexican-American President of the United States of America, someone with great poise and wit; a Mexican John F. Kennedy with a bristling moustache, who could stand up at a press conference of, say, 15,000 reporters and answer all questions in beautiful, fluent English, and then turn to the international reporters, the reporters from Spain and Argentina and Mexico, and point to one of them and say, *"¿Por favor, Señor Galindos, tiene pregunta?"*

Caballos smiled. Señor Presidente would begin his inauguration speech in Spanish, *"Queridos amigos . . ."* Or perhaps with, *"Ciudadanos . . ."* A bit formal there. Perhaps *"Queridos amigos"* would be best. Ah, what a perfect dream. A dark John F. Kennedy with a bristling moustache; a handsome Mexican who was composed, poised, full of grace and wit and charm and humor. His Mexican-American President would have a beautiful, clever wife; someone like Celine. She would stand up and make eloquent speeches and support important causes.

Someone behind him kicked his folding metal chair. Caballos's dream and smile faded. But who could possibly fulfill that dream? Who was there on the horizon or even in the shadows who could even come close to meeting that role? Who was there nationally? What happened to that guy from San Antonio, Texas; the one with the Ph.D.; the one that all Hispanics in the United States looked to for great political leadership? There had been so much hope there. What happened to him? Who was there locally? Who? Santamaría? Rafael Montoya? Sergio Barajas? Lord spare us. Leadership was embodied in egoists like the blond, blue-eyed Tito Torres who had his own agenda, the Latino Political Action Congress, a group he had founded. Tito made speeches that benefited a single constituency, the Latino Political Action Congress, nothing else. Tito attended the MAJA meetings on behalf of candidates or causes backed by his own group. Nothing else mattered to the cynical Tito. Or else there were well-intentioned people like Santamaría with kind hearts who—outside of a one-note Hispanic speech—were totally disorganized. Caballos looked at the windows filled with blackness hoping to see in the darkness some bright celestial hope, a Mexican Jesus, a dark JFK with a moustache. But there was no one, no one at all.

Caballos shifted and turned his gaze back to Victor Lopez. In all of this chaos perhaps there could be hope. Perhaps he was the one. It didn't *have* to be futile.

At the end of the MAJA meeting, when everyone was getting ready to reconvene for their sessions of fantasy and boasting at the Blackthorn, Señor Caballos approached Victor Lopez, shook his hand and said, "Victor, good to see you. Let's get together next week, *hombre*. No, not tonight, next week. I want to talk to you about something. Okay?"

"*Vale.*"

"*Vale.*"

Perhaps there was hope.

Driving home after the meeting, Caballos passed a group of boys standing on a bluff. As he passed them, each boy raised his arm and clenched his hand into a fist. The sight gave him hope: a group of boys waving at him, raising their clenched fists up to the air defiantly. There, he thought, there is the cream of our Hispanic youth, self-assured about their heritage, triumphant. Look at them, look at their dignity. So proud, so respectful of themselves. "There is a goodness and hope in my people," said Caballos, to no one in particular, to the steering wheel and dashboard of his car. What Caballos could not see—because of his astigmatism—was that from each fist protruded a single finger—the middle finger. All Caballos could see were the defiant upraised arms and clenched fists, not the boys giving him "the bird." Manny Caballos drove past the boys, smiling.

# The St. Michael The Archangel

"You Spanish punks are all alike. All you ever think of is nooky."

# 7. The Bvm, Joe, Mickey, Raef and Gabe

"*Mi hombre hermoso,*" she had said, whoever she had been, and Ruy Lopez was driven to frustration, for he could not identify the teasing woman who was now casting such a spell over him. He groped for her in the darkness of his own mind. And always the same ending: as others begin to strike matches around the hall, she escapes him. Curtain.

Who was she? Which one was she? How many times had she passed him on the street? How many times had she laughed at him? What torment. Later, while reading the paper or glancing at something, it would all be there again: the dance, the commotion, the sudden blackness, the hungry mouth at his lips, the small waist, the hair brushing his eyelids, and the yearning.

"*Mi hombre hermoso.*" My beautiful man, she had whispered, and then fled. Had it been real? Perhaps he had simply imagined it, the product of a fevered, tequila-and-champagne-induced imagining. But no sooner would he convince himself that it had only been a dream than it would play itself back vividly, and Ruy would once again be left dangling helplessly, longing for any kind of hint, the slightest clue to his spectacular phantom.

He would try not to think about her. He would dismiss the incident from his mind only to have it appear when he least expected it: the smell of vanilla, the starry darkness, the lips, the words, all there before him until he would hear the honking of a horn and he would find himself in an automobile stopped at an intersection before a green light as cars behind him would be blowing their horns.

"Hey, man, you in some kinda dream or something?" And, of course, he was.

Ruy snapped his fingers one day to signal the dawning of a great idea, a solution to his profound puzzle.

That was it. Of course. It was so simple. Ruy knew he had solved his great mystery. Or at least he thought so. It had to be Lourdes Pacheco, the wife of Conde Pacheco. That shy, tall beauty. Who else could it be? That splendid body. She was so reserved. He had danced with her at the wedding reception. Hadn't there been a bit of contact? A hint of promise? Who could predict the loneliness in a person's heart, the longing? Conde Pacheco was a jerk; everyone knew that. How could she stand him? Yes, that was it. It had to be Lourdes. She hungered for affection. That had to be it.

He would make his strategic move. He would plan it carefully, logically. He wouldn't rush it; let it play itself out naturally: a flowing stream, a sunrise, a blossoming flower, its petals slowly opening. It would be so beautiful. He would bring her out of her shyness. He could be very good at that. Perhaps he would do something as impulsive as what she had done, something fun, something silly. He would go see her, fling the door open and announce the presence of her Beautiful Man, her *hombre hermoso.* He'd do something lovely, something fun and spontaneous, and then the two of them would laugh and they'd tumble into each other's arms and kiss desperately, two human souls acknowledging their own humanity, their own frailties and fallibilities.

Yes, by God, he would do it. Soon.

*"Gracias, Diosito."*

He had finally solved his terrible puzzle.


A day later, Amapola gazed at her husband in disbelief.

"What happened, Ruy?"

"Never mind."

Amapola shook her head. "My God, it looks like you ran into a wild animal."

"I did. Two of them."

*"Hijo 'e la . . ."*

Amapola studied Ruy's black eye, a sore, extended lip, a blazing red nose. "Lost your temper again. *¿Verdad?*"

"No, I didn't lose my temper. I was very calm and cool."

"Somebody tried to cut you off in traffic and you called him a *pinchi-cabrón.* Right?"

"Wrong."

"As you were waiting in line somebody tried to push in front of you and you called him *chingado puto.* True?"

"False." Ruy was becoming irritated by Amapola's inquisition. *"Mira.* Do me a favor. Take a good look and then please shut up and leave me alone. O.K.? I feel bad enough as it is. *Por favor,* Amapola."

"Jesus, Ruy, you really should learn to control your temper."

. . .

That week there was great curiosity about Ruy's black eye, his swollen lip, his smashed nose. Ruy advanced several very believable explanations, which no one believed. Of course, the señoritas, Dolores and Lucrecia, were in ecstasy.

"Have you seen Ruy's face, Dolores?"

"But of course, *querida*. It looks like a pizza."

"Pepperoni and cheese."

"He claims it was an accident."

"I would not call Conde Pacheco's fists an accident."

"Neither would I."

"They say she hit him on the head."

"With a frying pan."

"A rolling pin."

"No, I hear it was a frying pan."

"I'm sorry, dear, it was a rolling pin."

"*Ya que,* whatever . . ."

"While Conde was kicking him in the stomach."

"I hear it was a little lower than that."

"Indecent."

"Disgusting."

"How terrible."

"How horrible."

"I feel so sorry for Amapola, Ruy's dear wife."

"She is so loyal to that pig."

"She must be so embarrassed."

"So embarrassed."

"Can you blame her?"

"What these filthy men will not do for sex."

"Strange sex."

"Disgusting sex."

"Indecent sex."

"Disgusting pigs."

"It is the will of God."

"So be it."

*"Ave María Purísima."*

*"Sea por Dios."*

Ruy's dilemma was now compounded by injury and, most painful of all, ridicule. To say the least, his carefully plotted plan had been less than successful. Lourdes had not appreciated Ruy's spontaneous demonstration of spontaneous love. Neither had her husband, Conde Pacheco.

Through a blackened eye, Ruy peeked at the dim daylight and whispered, "Lourdes Pacheco was not the one." He tried to explain his "accident" to anyone who would listen. "So, a guy makes a little mistake and everybody acts so cute about it. Why does everyone think black eyes are so funny anyway?"

Such was Ruy's misery that he even tried praying. On Sunday, in church, he looked up at the statue of St. Anthony, the patron saint of lost causes, crossed himself and began to pray. But the only words he could utter were *"Mi hombre hermoso."* What kind of a prayer was that?

Even now, as he begged for an answer to his puzzle, she was probably there in one of the pews, smiling, mocking him, perhaps even laughing. Ruy looked up at the enormous crucifix over the main altar and uttered in despair, "Who is she?" from the very pit of his soul, as that little dwarf, Eufemio Galian, turned in the pew ahead of Ruy, placed an index finger across his lips, inhaled and issued a long, hissing "Shhhhhhhh," as if blowing out candles on a birthday cake. Eufemio Galian also informed Ruy that he had a black eye.

Ruy informed Eufemio that he should shut his trap and Eufemio began to cry and then his mother asked Ruy if he would like another black eye to match the one he already had, an offer Ruy politely declined.

Ruy even tried praying to the Blessed Virgin Mary.

"Please, *Virgensita,* tell me who she is," and his reverential eyes went up to the blue and white statue. He studied the statue carefully, the slender waist, the fingers, the sweet repose, the small lips, and then, incredibly, inconceivably, in Ruy's constant drifting daydream, her small, dainty fingers began to hold his own erection, and he began to wonder what it'd be like French-kissing the Blessed Virgin Mary, what she'd be like in bed. What she'd say afterwards. Maybe she'd have a cigarette. Be grateful. Have a nice chat.

"Thanks, hon. Wow, that was terrific. I like it when you do that to me, talk dirty to me that way," she would say, inhaling a mentholated cigarette. "I like it when you call me a filthy bitch, a rotten whore, a dirty slut," she would add, blowing out a plume of cigarette smoke and then removing a speck of tobacco from the tip of her tongue with a long crimson fingernail.

"You're probably wondering how I got into this whole gig; most of the guys do. I want to tell you something. It was no big deal. I mean one day this archangel comes down from Heaven and scares the living shit out of me and says, 'O.K., sister, you're it.' I didn't know what the guy was talking about. You know, 'O.K., sister, you're it.' I mean here's this guy with these wings—I mean I'm talking *wings;* about a twenty-foot wingspan—and he's giving me this 'you're it' bit.

"So I says, 'I'm it? Excuse me? What do you mean by

that crack? What are we doing, playing tag?' I was still pissed by the way he scared me.

"And he says, 'You're going to be the Mother of God.'

"I mean *come on.* Give me a *break.* I'm just this kid and this guy in drag wearing a dress and wings is telling me that I'm going to be the Mother of God. I mean like Wow! He tells me that he's serious and shows me his flaming sword like I mean that's *really* going to turn me on. I mean if it were like a real rad Corvette or fab Jag or something. You know? But he tries to impress me with this sword and he begins to torch a bunch of bushes all around me. Like the guy is going nuts. I mean he is *absolutely* out of *control.* He's pulling this big Mr. Terminator bit on me and I ask him why he's nuking the bushes. You should have seen the smoke and mess he was creating; Pollution City. I mean like he goes ballistic; I mean like he's going *totally* ballistic.

"He tells me I had been chosen and that I could not pass up the opportunity of a lifetime to start up a new religion and to change the world. I mean like Wow! Give me a break. I mean like give me a fucking ber-*rake.* I couldn't shake him so I decided I'd play along with it just for laughs and maybe get rid of the dweeb. What did I have to lose?

"So I says, 'BFD, if I *were* to do this Mother of God bit, and I'm not saying I will, but if I were to become the Mother of God what's in it for Número Uno? What's in it for me?' I could hardly keep a straight face.

"And you know what he tells me? 'Your reward will be timeless, universal and eternal.' I mean like, Whoa, define your terms, buster.

" 'But, honey,' I says, 'that's not going to put the lasagna on María's table. Besides, the words "Timeless" and "Eternal" are redundant.' But it's like he's not listening; he can't hear a *thing* I'm saying. And then, get this, he tells me that I'll become a saint and that they'll build churches in my name throughout the world and that they will write a prayer and a battle strategy and a football play called the Hail Mary in my honor plus a whole bunch of music not to mention the perks I would get in Heaven for being the Mother of God. Big limo, cellular phone, hot tub, my own masseur, free dental plan. I couldn't get him out of my face. He was beginning to sound like a commercial for a hemorrhoid ointment. But by and by I started to listen. I mean I *really* started to listen. I liked the part about the limo and some of the perks he mentioned and the idea of being part of a new Italian start-up company although I probably would have called it something else. I never did care for the names they chose: 'Catholicism.' 'The Catholic Church.' 'Holy Mother Church.' 'The one, true, holy, Catholic, apostolic and universal church,' whatever that means. A lot of it was La-La, blah-blah-blah brochure hype.

"This cherub dude *had* to be in sales. He kept right on coming at me with The Deal. I could just picture him putting the make on some Sheila. He was really kind of cute. He'd probably score except for the haircut and that drag costume he was wearing. I mean, Dumbo City.

"What began to sway me was the idea of all of the songs and music they would write about me; but I guess what really did it was when he mentioned all of the cool clothes I could wear, in particular my favorite colors which are blue and white. I've had my colors done. You like my eyeliner and mascara? Isn't it bitchin'?

"This angel guy then tells me, 'O.K., you're all set. In a

few days you will meet St. Joseph. He doesn't know he's going to be canonized but we've got it wired. He is a holy man who will assist you with your immaculate conception.'

" 'Negative, Burning Sword. You're breaking up. I cannot read you. My immaculate *what?*'

" 'Your immaculate conception.'

" 'Say again.'

" 'Immaculate conception.'

" 'Explain.'

" 'The birth of the Son of God must be pure. He must be conceived in an immaculate way.'

" 'Sex doesn't have to be dirty, honey.'

" 'You don't understand.'

" 'You've got to be kidding, Smoky. Do you mean to tell me I'm supposed to give birth to this God guy without having sex? No guy? No sex?'

" 'No guy. No sex.'

" 'No way! You mean I can't fool around?'

" 'That's right.'

" 'Not even just a teense?'

" 'Not even just a teense.'

" 'No way, René,' I said. 'If I'm going to have a kid I at least want to have a little fun in the process.' I was about to tell this guy to chuck it, but he kept telling me about the perks. I think it was the masseur that did it—I get this nasty soreness in my neck all the time. And don't forget, I was *so* young, *so* impressionable—your basic big-chested, stupid, fertile María with the big nose. I finally told him that I'd do it on four conditions.'

" 'What's that?' he says.

" '(A) that I get a complete list of the perks *in writing*

signed by the head honcho himself. I mean like the Main Man.'

" 'No problemo.'

" '(B) that you guys pay to have my nose bobbed.'

" 'You got it.'

" '(C) that no one, I mean no one, ever finds out that I had this kid without having sex.'

" 'And . . . ?'

" 'And (D) that when it's all over I get to party with my choice of any stud or studs on the ranch. I get my pick of the litter. *Comprende?*'

" 'Done deal.'

" 'Cross your heart?'

" 'Cross my heart and hope to die.' Which sounded pretty good at the time until I later realized, 'Yo. Hey, wait a minute. This dude's an angel. He's already dead.' Needless to say the facts of the birth went public. My agent absolutely insisted on it. It made great promotion copy and now you find the term 'Immaculate Conception' everywhere. I mean on *everything.* Part of The Deal.

"But I'm going to tell you something. It wasn't any picnic. This guy Joe—excuse me, St. Joseph—was hell to live with. He was never a very good carpenter to begin with and he simply would *not* let me get *near* him, no matter how sexy I felt. Wouldn't lay a finger on me. I used to tell him, 'Joe, *come on,* honey, who's going to know? Don't you ever get horny?' And he would say, 'I cannot, in good conscience, allow you to talk that way.' What a drag. He'd always lower his voice like that whenever he wanted to treat me like a child, 'I cannot in good conscience . . .' Christ, half the time he sounded like my dad. I was beginning to think the guy was like *gay* except that later on I found out he had signed this *beaucoup* deal for Very Big Bucks for not touching me. He got a whole bunch of money up front, a place on the coast plus a twenty-percent royalty on every Bible and rosary ever sold. Not bad. Run the numbers on that one, Donald. Made my own deal look like chicken feed.

"But, God, he could be so obstinate. When I was pregnant with the kid, he *insisted* on taking this trip. He wanted to go to Bethlehem, of all places, for his high school reunion. I told him, 'Joe, come on already. I'm due anytime now. Please, baby, can't we just stay home and watch a burning bush? We can go to your reunion next year.' But he wouldn't listen. So here we are wandering all over Bethlehem, I'm preggers and about to pop at any moment, we hardly have a cent to our name, all we have to get around is this stupid animal from Rent-a-Burro and we can't even find a place to sleep. I mean wasn't that stupid? I think there was some sort of convention going on in Bethlehem. I mean you couldn't find a place *anywhere*. So we end up in this barn where I had the kid. Oh, sure, the book calls it a 'manger' and they make it all sound so wonderful and romantic. That's something the marketing firm —MML&J (Matthew, Mark, Luke, and John)—did to give the story what they called a 'human interest spin.' They changed barn to manger and changed the three retards that were lost to, get this, the Three Wise Men. Believe it. If they were so wise what were they doing wandering around in the desert following some dumb star on a cold December night? Right? Makes you wonder. Should have named them Larry, Curly and Moe.

"And you've seen those paintings with all of those shepherds and beautiful animals radiating this big holy glow as they look at the newborn babe? It's all bullshit. I don't think the shepherds ever took baths, the whole place stank to high heaven. And it was really, really cold. I mean it's December twenty-fifth out in some barn. My tootsies were *far-reezing*. It's not as if we're in some big fancy Hilton Hotel with heat and room service and cable TV. Joe was no help. He got all sappy and stupid. Spent what little money we had left on Southern Comfort, his favorite drink. Do you know what he tells me? 'Mary-Jo.' (God I hated that name.) 'Mary-Jo, relax, babes, come on,' he says. 'Hey, ease it up, loosen up, chill out. I'm just celebrating the holidays.' And he gives me this stupid, mushy grin. I think he would've hit on me and blown his contract had I not just given birth to Junior.

"As for the kid, he wasn't exactly any barrel of monkeys either. I mean here you've got this kid who's God. Right? And I'm going to tell him to eat his mush? Yeah.

" 'Eat your mush, killer, and you'll grow up to be big and strong like God the Father who goes around scaring the living shit out of people.' Yeah, right. He had a real smart mouth too. I'd ask him to clean up his room and he'd tell me, 'My kingdom is not of this world.'

" 'I don't give a shit. Just clean up your room!'

"God, he could make me so mad. I should have slapped that sass right out of his punk mouth. When I'd upset him, though, he'd get this funny look and all I could think of was that other dude that went around nuking bushes with his flaming sword. So I pretty much let the kid do what he wanted. A real pain in the you-know-what. Went around talking about the Sacred Trinity, the Communion of Saints, the Forgiveness of Sins. *Bore-ring.*

"The kid's name gave us a *lot* of trouble. I wanted to call him Chauncey after a favorite uncle and Joe wanted to call him Geordie, which I thought sounded *really* phony. Isn't that a dumb name? I mean can you imagine people praying to Geordie or trying to sing it? 'Oh-oh, Lo-o-ordy, Geordie, Make the Goo-ood Times Roll, Pray-ay-sed be Thy Ho-oh, Owa Holy Name, Gee-oh-ho-ho-hor-dee.' Sheeet. For a while we just called the kid Junior. One day Joe was in his studio— I think they called it a carpenter's shop in the book—and he's hammering this box together and I know, I just know what's going to happen next. So I said, 'Joe, be careful, sweetie, you're bringing that hammer awfully close to your pinkie.' And he gives me this real nasty look and says, 'Look, I'll make a little deal with you. I don't tell you how to be the Mother of God and raise Junior, you don't tell me how to do carpentry. O.K.?' he says real smart-alecky like. And sure enough, with the next blow, the very next blow, he brings the hammer down on his thumb. I mean right *on top* of his thumb. Ouch! It was black-and-blue for weeks. Joe was so pissed. I told you he was a shitty carpenter. And he yells out, get this, 'Jesus Christ!' And we both looked at each other and I started to laugh. 'What a crazy name to give the kid,' I yelled. Honestly, I couldn't stop laughing. Isn't that a stitch? Naming the kid after something a guy yells when he hits his thumb with a hammer? I mean was that just *too much?* I was just kidding, of course, but the name stuck. I don't think Junior ever did like it, and he was absolutely livid when I told him the true story of his name. He had like *zero* sense of humor. Wouldn't speak to me for days except to ask, 'How many angels on the head of a pin?' And I'd say, 'Beats the shit out of me. How should I know? Go ask Smoky with the flaming sword.' He even went around using the name 'Jay' for a while. Sounded *so* affected.

You probably know most of the rest. The Apostles. The Crucifixion. Pontius Pilate. Easter. The Rolling Stone. The miracle stuff was a lot of B.S. thrown in by MML&J. Anyway, this is getting boring. Let's fuck. I'm getting horny again. By the way, can I ask you a teensy-weensy favor?"

"Of course," said Ruy.

"Would you embugger me?"

"I'm sorry?"

"Oh, you know . . . Cripes. How else *would* you put it? I'm trying not to be crude. Would you mind putting it where the sun don't shine?"

Ruy hesitated. "I'm sorry, I still don't . . ."

"Look, get with the program. Don't Mexicans ever do that? God, you're almost as bad as Joe. Would you mind sticking your sweet shlong up my tushie?"

"No, no, of course not."

"Thanks, hon, you're a doll. You know you *really* know how to turn a girl on. Let's do the whole thing. Don't hold back on me. Pork me. Hurt me. Eat me raw. Treat me like scum. I love the rough stuff. Where did you ever learn to do that? I mean like, Wow! None of the other guys ever does that to me or talks to me that way. 'Dirty bitch. Filthy slut.' I love it. You know, it really pisses me off. They all think I'm so pure and innocent, you know, a virgin. When you've got a name like the BVM, you know, the Blessed Virgin Mary . . ."

Hey, wait a minute!

The Big T. Time Out! Twrreeet!

What the hell's going on?

Holy Mother of God!

Can you believe what Ruy was thinking? Sex with the Sacred, the Most Blessed Virgin Mary, the Holy Mother of God? In a Catholic church? In a Catholic Hell those thoughts would cast him into a titanic, fiery pit of sulfur for All Eternity. Dante's Inferno does not possess a ring low enough in Hell for that kind of blasphemy. At the very least Ruy's thoughts would banish him to purgatory for approximately two billion years, or until either the Boston Red Sox or the Chicago Cubs win a World Series, whichever comes first. They would be worth a major share of plenary indulgences on the open market. "Hey, buddy, c'mere. Looking for a deal on a plenary indulgence?"

Ruy crossed himself and said a Hail Mary and a Quick Confiteor before he could die and burn in Hell for All Eternity. If you didn't say a Quick Confiteor, with all of that on your soul, forget it. He asked forgiveness for his blasphemous thoughts. That's all he needed: to upset herself, the BVM, the Blessed Virgin Mary. All she had to do was buzz Michael, Gabriel and Raphael on the cellular telephone in her limousine and the next thing you'd know the three archangels would be paying him a little social visit:

"Hi, handsome."

"Hi."

"Mr. Low-pay?"

"Lopez."

"Yes. Lopez. Hi. My name's Michael and these here's my partners, Gabe and Rafe. We're archangels."

"Archangels? ¡Aiii, Diosito!" Ruy would gasp, his voice cracking, as the three archangels shoved past him.

"Uh, listen, man, we were sent here by the BVM, you know what I mean? A little bit of business."

"Hey, *dick-head!*" Michael would yell, clapping his hands.

"Anybody home?" Raphael would say, snapping his fingers.

"*Capisce?*" Gabriel would scream.

Ruy would snap out of it. "Yes-yes-yes."

"We'd like to have a little chat with you."

"Fine. Sure. Woe-woe-won't you have some coffee? Do archangels drink coffee?"

"No thanks, man, we don't drink that shit."

"Keeps us awake nights. Know what I mean? Ha."

"Ha. That's good, Mickey."

"Ha-ha-ha?" asked Ruy.

"You think something's funny, bright boy?"

"We make you laugh?"

"We got funny pictures tattooed on the end of our noses?"

"Oh-no-no-no-sir."

"Well then, shut the fuck up."

"Yes, sir."

"Sit it down, man."

"You understand English, man? Mickey said, 'Sit it down!'" Gabriel would say, shoving Ruy into a chair and slapping him with a wing.

"Do you mind if we close the door?" Raphael would ask. "This could get a little hairy."

"Know what we mean?"

"Tense?"

"Ya-yes. Sssss . . . s-s-sir. Look. I know why you're here. I'm sorry. I can explain everything. It was all a terrible misunderstanding. I couldn't help what I was thinking in church the other day. You see, I'm Mexican. That sort of explains everything. That's all there was to it."

"Bullshit!" acknowledged St. Raphael the Archangel.

"Shut the fuck up!" explained St. Michael the Archangel.

"We'll do the talking," clarified St. Gabriel.

"You think you're pretty cute, don't you? 'This guy in drag wearing a dress and wings . . .' "

"Bastard."

" 'This cherub dude . . .' "

"Dick-head!"

" 'Pork me. Hurt me. Eat me raw. Treat me like scum.' "

"Ass-wipe."

" 'Smoky with the burning sword.' "

"Shit-for-brains."

St. Raphael would slap Ruy across the face with a wing as St. Michael would unsheathe a flaming sword.

"Ever seen one of these before, smart fuck?"

Ruy would gasp at the sight of the flaming sword. "*¡Aiii, Diosito! ¡Aiii, Diosito mío!*"

"Too late, Pan-choe."

"Not that one, Mickey," Raphael would say, and Michael would push the sword and scabbard aside and begin to screw a silencer on the barrel of a .22-caliber pistol. "How about the 'shredder' this time, Mickey? It's more painful."

"Yeah, you're right," Michael would say, pulling out a sawed-off shotgun from one of his wings. "The shredder's more painful."

"Right in the face. Shove it right into his fucking Mexican mouth."

"Say 'ahhh,' bright boy."

Ruy would throw himself on the floor and hug Michael's

knees and plead, "Please, please, I am not an evil man. Please. Give me another chance. Don't you understand? I couldn't *help* myself. I'm *Mexican!*"

"I guess that's supposed to excuse everything."

"Please! Please! Have mercy on me."

"Bullshit! You Spanish punks are all alike. All you ever think of is nooky. Now you're even thinking of hitting on the Blessed Virgin Mary, the Mother of God. Jesus H. Jones, you make me want to puke."

"Disgusting bastard."

"Get up off the floor, dick-head, and take it like a man. You revolting scum, you make me sick. Look at the son-of-a-bitch grovel. You pissed off the BVM and now you're going to pay for it, asshole. Go ahead, Mickey, blow him away."

*"Ker-chow!"*


Ruy shuddered, crossed himself again, said another Quick Confiteor and asked for forgiveness for his sins and for the salvation of his immortal soul as well as for mercy from the Blessed Mother and her three hit archangels, Mickey, Rafe and Gabe.

And then in his ongoing bewilderment, strange things began to happen to Ruy. Lulusa, his haughty beagle-mix dog, was baying at the moon. ("Dogs bay at the moon when they see the Devil," according to Señorita Lucrecia.) The following day, his wife, Amapola, appeared, framed in a doorway, wearing a silly black and pink teddy and high-heeled shoes. Large, dear Amapola, loyal and warm as cocoa. And Ruy, overwhelmed with longing, tried but could not satisfy his dear, fat wife who finally turned her back on him and sobbed quietly.

Can you believe it? Ruy, who placed such a premium on *machismo*, was unable to fulfill the most basic and primitive of all husbandly duties. Can you possibly believe it? *"Aiii, Diosito, Diosito mío,"* said Ruy, convinced that he was losing his manhood. Perhaps he was turning into a *maricón*. The thought of having to hang around YMCA rest rooms to find a small fragment of love or affection made him cringe.

Extraordinary things were happening.

Time began to layer over Ruy's great Mexican Grief. Perhaps it could soon be forgotten.

Until he began receiving those notes.

They were exquisite notes; the parchment paper smelled of vanilla; the handwriting was beautiful; the notes always began, *"Mi Hombre Hermoso."* They went into great detail in describing Ruy's blue eyes, his dark hair, his stocky build, his full lips, his complexion.

The odor of vanilla was an elation and a depression. It was the aroma that had embraced him in darkness that fateful night, the night of the wedding reception. And here it was all back again. Totally. Instantly.

Those impossible notes. These were followed by lovely gifts, pleasant surprises. Who was doing it? Who was doing this to him? Who was writing these elaborate letters in Spanish and English filled with imaginative phrases, wit, learning? Who was it? They were lovely, perfect notes, as exquisite as the handwriting, bearing the aroma of vanilla; the odor that was filling his nights with longing and his days with despair. And always the memory of the night, that night and that dewy neck, the slim waist.

"Oh, my God," sighed Ruy. It took nothing at all to re-create the madness. Every note brought it all back. Every note hinted of intrigue and profound possibilities. Why was she doing this? Surely it was meant to drive him to madness. Surely it could not go on or he would be placed in a darkened room where he could peacefully and at his own leisurely pace beat the contents of his head into a nice Mexican *salsa cruda.*

That exquisite handwriting. The capital letter "G" climbed up into an elegant loop, swung across into a smaller loop, and then descended into a swirling finale. To Ruy, whose own handwriting was atrocious, that letter alone was a perfect small song, a graceful dance step. Those letters produced an elation followed by an almost unbearable frustration. Why was this woman, so articulate, whose handwriting was delicate and perfect, why was she taunting him with these gifts and intimate, finely crafted notes? He felt he was being observed, an insect or animal in someone's preposterous experiment. But why? His mother would have said simply, *"Sea por Dios."* If only he had his mother's blind faith he could reduce all things to a simple formula and a single sentence, "It is the Will of God." But no sooner would he be ready to accept what was happening to him than his eyes would close and his mouth would tighten and he would feel her lips and embrace her body and hear the phrase once again, *"Mi hombre hermoso."*

And he would read those notes, reread them and then reread them yet again.

*Sea por Dios.* It was the Will of God.

# 8. A Very Big Deal

Up went the comb, up; the left hand followed the comb, up to the top and then across. Damy Taggart was looking into the mirror as he combed his hair. He looked at himself from the right side and then the left, staring, always staring, at the golden smoothness of a well-trimmed blond beard and then into the milky depth of his own baby-blue eyes.

Damy curled his upper lip, spat out the words "Come get me, baby." He was addressing no one, everyone, every woman that lusted for him, that wanted him as he stood there in the men's room of the La Lunita Restaurant, arms akimbo, feet apart. What woman could possibly resist this devastating blond, blue-eyed macho dripping with testosterone. There wasn't a woman in the country, in the world, who could possibly resist this nitroglycerine keg of manhood that could go off with the slightest provocation. Damy looked down, lowered his head and then slowly swept his eyes up to look at himself. It was "The Look," Damy's infamous "Look of Devastation," his own term.

Certain professional athletes boast—in writing—of their thousands of sexual conquests. Damy preferred not to keep score. His logic was that it would be unfair to the girls he had not yet seduced to keep that kind of record. Besides, Damy didn't just "do" sex—as in "doing" lunch—Damy Made Love, a subtle but important distinction. "Oh, baby, I could love you," he said, echoing a female whisper he had recently heard.

Damy's demeanor changed. He suddenly barked out, "What did you call me?" He was now Damy the Bad. He snarled at his image in the mirror. "It's your choice. You can either have instant death," said Damy, holding up his right fist to the mirror, "or ten months in the hospital." He was taunting an unfortunate, imaginary trespasser, holding up his left fist. "I'm going to teach you a little lesson you will never forget, punk."

And then back to Damy Testosterone. He lowered his voice, "Honey, come get me. I've got what you want: eleven inches of swinging peter." As with most Mission District statistics, Damy's numbers were exaggerated. A general rule of thumb in dealing with Mission District statistics is to divide any number presented by a factor of 2.3.

Up once again went the comb, up slow and smooth and languid; across the left side of his greasy blond hair and then over to the right. Down and across and then two sensuous swipes across each side. Here was a man, The *Man*: Mr. Double Cool himself, Damy Superb, Damy the Devastator. We all have our share of burdens; Damy's was his greasy good looks which he enhanced with an undersized, tight shirt open to the middle of his chest—where a crucifix hung from a gold chain—and a black leather jacket which hid his small, white arms and thin muscles. All the muscle Damy needed was there in his jacket pocket, an easily concealable 9mm automatic pistol.

Damy looked at himself from the left, the right, the left, the right. He ran the comb through a handsome beard that was so blond it almost looked golden. When Damy was satisfied, he slipped his comb into the pocket of a pair of baggy black pants. And then, with his thumb, he added a crease to a wave of hair over his forehead. It was art, the final, perfect touch, the maraschino cherry on top of the dollop of whipped cream. He tucked at his collar, stuck out his neck, licked his lips and flung open the bathroom door. Like the consummate actor that he was, he was ready to go back onstage, back to his table at La Lunita Restaurant.

He returned to the table to find that the meal he had ordered—*chiles rellenos,* rice and beans—had been served. He looked up to see that Conde Pacheco had entered the restaurant. Damy turned to avoid making contact with Conde.

"Jesus Christ, Damy, am I glad to see you. I gotta talk to you, man," said Conde, pulling a chair away from Damy's table and straddling it quickly. As usual, Conde Pacheco was in a terrible hurry. He acted like an escaped convict who had a fifteen-minute lead on his pursuers.

"What's up?"

"Damy, my friend, this is not Conde Pacheco talking, this is opportunity knocking," Conde said, licking his lips. The excessive grin appeared, the exposed teeth, the wide mouth. Damy looked up to be met by pink gums, molars, incisors, an exorbitant moustache and a large, sharp nose. "Deals like this do not come along every day of the week."

A bottle of beer, tortilla chips and *salsa jalapeño* were

brought to the table. Conde helped himself, taking several chips and dipping one in the salsa.

Damy eyed Conde suspiciously. "What's the deal?"

"Listen, man, I got a terrific deal for you on some designer jeans. You won't believe this one. They're perfect. I just got 'em. You know what I mean? They're beautiful. Whadyou say?"

Damy put down his fork, carefully wiped his lips, swallowed, took a sip of beer. "You mean like that terrific deal you gave me on those Rolex watches?"

"Oh, man. Come on. That was a long time ago. Bygones are bygones? How did I know they were fakes from Thailand? This stuff's gorgeous. The women love 'em. Shows off their buns. Whadyou say?"

"Thank you very much, Conde. I appreciate your offer. We have been good friends for a while now . . ."

"Oh, man, don't give me that. You want to talk or make speeches? This stuff's perfect. I'm giving you first ups."

"Why me?"

"Because we've done a lot of business. Look, the jeans are so good you can unload them in fifteen minutes. It's the real thing. Trust me."

Damy took a mental note of the location of his wallet; he had a tendency to do so whenever Conde said, "Trust me."

"How many?"

"Three hundred."

"Where'd you get 'em?"

"Oh, you know, the usual."

Damy picked the napkin off his lap, wiped his mouth and took a swig of beer. "Conde, I've gotta tell you something. I am now closing the sweetest deal of my life."

"What are you doing? Loans?"

"No, not loans. I can't tell you, Conde."

"What is it? Smashing cars and collecting the insurance?"

Damy laughed. "No, no, not cars, not loans. All of that stuff's a thing of the past. I can't go into details, Conde, but it looks so good I could be sitting very pretty for the rest of my life." Damy covered his mouth, burped softly.

"Couldn't you give me just a little hint? If it's so good maybe we could, you know, work on it together; maybe a guy could get into it with you, you know, help you out a little, become your partner."

Damy laughed. "No thanks, Conde. I can't cut you in on this. See that car out there?" Damy pointed to a shiny red Corvette parked in front of the restaurant. "My new business is responsible for that. How many jeans do you suppose I'd have to sell to come up with that kind of cash?"

"Dope. You're doing dope. Someone told me you were now into dope. It's true, isn't it?"

"There can be a lot of money in it if you do it right; if you don't get caught."

"If you don't get caught. You can also get yourself into a lot of trouble."

"Let me worry about that, Conde. O.K.?"

"I take it you don't want the jeans then? They're not real 'hot' or anything. You know?"

"Conde, I've gone beyond selling stolen jeans."

Conde relaxed, sat back, took a swig of Damy's beer.

"Besides jeans, what are you doing now, Conde? Are you still fixing traffic tickets?"

"I'm working for Supervisor von Meisterding."

"That's what I thought. You're still flacking for 'Meester.'"

"I'm a facilitator."

"What does that mean, besides fixing traffic tickets?"

"I make it worth Meester's time to see and be involved with people from the Mission District."

"Is there any money in that?"

"It pays the bills. People who want something from Meester come to me. If he wants something from them he goes through me. It works both ways. I work on a commission. I also have a few other things going, like, you know?"

"Like jeans?"

"Yeah, whatever. That and the other stuff."

A dull electronic ringing could be heard. Damy reached into his jacket and pulled out a cellular telephone.

"Yeah? Hi. Uh-huh." Damy was looking directly at Conde Pacheco. "Right. Good. How much? You serious? Wow! I'll take care of it."

Damy put the telephone away. "I gotta run, Conde," he said, snapping his fingers for the bill. "I'll talk to you soon."

"You're doing dope, aren't you, Damy?"

Damy turned and glanced over his shoulder. "Hey," he said as he exited the restaurant.

"O.K., O.K.," said Conde, grabbing a tortilla off of Damy's plate. And he was gone, still ahead of his pursuers.

# 9. A Hand Appears

A hand appears, burgundy fingernail polish, and then a female face, with much makeup, burgundy lipstick. A hand and then a face: silvery eye shadow, long eyelashes. Lined eyebrows, metallic rouge. She looks unreal. When she sits motionless, staring at a distant object, she turns into a mannequin, a painting. The illusion disappears when she moves, when she bows her head slowly and begins combing her hair. Her movements are slow, easy. Ruy smiles. Why does the sight of a woman combing her hair suddenly turn into an immortal gesture, right here in a donut shop on Mission Street? When the combing is finished, she extracts a pair of oversized dark glasses from a large purse, wraps them across her face, and once again she becomes something unreal: metallic and strange: Ruy's eternal female fantasy. Yet again, a beautiful woman, a voluptuous houri, always so close and yet impossible to touch? Ruy smelled her perfume as she walked by, as she walked out, out of the coffee shop and out of his life, never to be seen again.

Or a voice.

A familiar voice calls out. *"¡Epa, mano!* Ruy, are you all right? *¿Qué te pasa, mano?"*

Ruy wandered aimlessly, hopelessly, through his maze of longing. Objects, faces, would appear and disappear as if in a desert glaze or a sun's glare on an evening lake. Familiar things appeared behind sun-reflecting windows. Occasionally, a face would appear out of that glare.

A hand came across a table, a white hand with long painted fingernails. Ruy was startled at the sudden appearance of the ivory-like hand. He looked up to see Mrs. Birdwell. She was near him and yet, as she stared off into the distance, she appeared as if out of yet another dream.

A cup and saucer were extended to Ruy. Holding the cup was that hand with perfect fingers almost as white as the linen tablecloth. It was a fine, white hand with tiny blue veins and dark fingernails. Ruy awoke from a daydream of flowers whose petals opened and closed quickly. He looked up to see Mrs. Birdwell pouring tea into his cup. It was a ceremony Mrs. Birdwell performed with great dignity—the heating of the water, the preparation of the tea, the pouring of the hot water, the steeping. Ruy wondered why she couldn't just buy tea bags or instant coffee like everyone else instead of having to go through so much rigamarole. Ruy was as puzzled about this as about several other things in his life which he could not fathom. He could not satisfy his own wife, he was being taunted by some woman that smelled of vanilla, and yesterday Lulusa, his dog, had offered him a dead lizard. The dog's brown eyes had sparkled as she had placed the lizard at Ruy's feet and looked up at him with a look of unbounded tenderness.

Strange, all strange. But strangest of all, there he was holding hands with Mrs. Birdwell. There he was once again, in the Birdwell mansion, going through this strange ceremonial thing with Mrs. Birdwell in which she spoke of mature affections and discriminating emotions, and occasionally reached over to pat his head as if he were an obedient Mexican spaniel, which, of course, he was. His mystery woman continued to taunt him. The last thing Ruy needed now was additional discreet complications. But he could hardly afford to lose the Birdwell place. Mrs. Birdwell had slipped her foot out of her shoe and was stroking his calf with her toes. Ruy swallowed. Another bit of proper New England sex was at hand. Another lemon cupcake or egg salad sandwich on white bread with mayonnaise.

# 10. An Ominous Sign

A row of spears pointing skyward was, in reality, a large wrought-iron gate in the driveway of the two-story red and gray house on Glenwood and Nineteenth streets. A row of upward-pointing arrows—a short wrought-iron fence and gate —lined the tiny front yard which consisted of little more than a concrete path and a small flower bed. Dominating the front yard was an exorbitant banana tree whose arching leaves towered above the tiled roof of the house and an out-of-control camellia plant the size of a tree. Both plants produced a constant shower of odorous decay. Completing the florid richness were two large sidewalk bottlebrush trees in full bloom and a rusting red Buick on the street with two flat tires.

From the outside, the house appeared tranquil and serene. But inside, the first signs of turmoil were becoming apparent.

Molly the cat and Lulusa the dog snapped awake.

"Son-of-a-bitch," screamed Ruy Lopez, and suddenly the legs of the tables became weak and spindly, the walls became very thin, a coffee table appeared very fragile. One could almost see these objects bracing themselves, crossing themselves, praying to be spared. The entire house seemed to be shuddering.

Lulusa moved away from a passageway to a neutral corner, under a bed where she would be secure and out of reach. Molly flipped an eyelid open and took a precise reading. She carefully assessed the situation: the volume of Ruy's voice, the stomping, the slamming, and got up quickly from her sunny perch and stretched. If only Ruy's wife, Amapola, were here. She would temper Ruy's temper. Instead Amapola was visiting her Auntie Rosalía in Sacramento and wouldn't be back until later that day.

When she saw Lulusa walking by very determined, very businesslike, Molly decided that the jig was up. Molly would spend the rest of the day with Cheap Thrills, a harmless calico cat, an old neutered friend whose nice master was Señora Talavera. The old woman was a little batty perhaps but that didn't matter. Her cooking was superb and besides she was a soft touch. All one had to do was purr a little, rub up against her ankles, and Señora Talavera would produce a fine piece of marinated chicken or a glass of room-temperature milk. Her turkey in *mole* sauce was to die for. Surely it would one day be declared a national or perhaps even an international legacy, a United Nations World Heritage Recipe. Ruy screamed again. Time was wasting. Time to hightail it out of here.

There comes a point when anger becomes madness. For Ruy that moment had arrived. An ominous sign had flown into Ruy's life. A bird had flown into Ruy's home that morning—a blackbird. Ruy saw this as a terrific omen, a Heaven-sent warning.

"¡*Madre de Dios!*"

Not that Ruy was superstitious. After all, superstition was for old ladies and those awful *metichis,* Señorita Lucrecia and Señorita Dolores, with their herbal remedies and laxatives and enemas. That was all for nincompoops and the superstitious. It was just that there were certain signs one could not avoid. It was a sign, a definite sign of an impending disaster. For a perfect, peaceful moment, Ruy looked at the bird flying frantically inside the house. Ruy smiled. He would get the bird, remove the threat. He wondered whether to open all of the windows and doors in order to let the bird out. And then he wondered whether to close all the doors and windows so that other dark birds couldn't get in. Ruy picked up a broom and pursued the evil omen. He knew it. He could tell. He could sense it. Dark things were about to happen. Ruy, in his shorts and undershirt, armed with a broom, chased the blackbird. He swung at the bird and it began squawking wildly.

"Son-of-a-bitch," screamed Ruy. And to think that only minutes earlier the bird had been flying through the blue sky with some old friends singing a happy tune, counting his blessings, happy to be alive. "Shucks, Maury, look at that view, smell that air. Isn't it great to be a bird? Makes you glad to be alive."

Such were the bird's happy thoughts before entering the home of Ruy Lopez. And now look at him, fearing for his life as some madman chased him with a broom. But life was like that sometimes. You could never predict exactly when a Mexican wearing shorts was going to chase you with a broom.

Ruy kept swinging away at the poor bird, his nemesis, a dark, evil sign. What did the bird—his name was Ralph— really care about signs and omens? He happened to be black simply because his mother and father were black. He couldn't help it if others saw this as evil and offensive. If your mother and father are blackbirds what else can you be but a blackbird? Can you imagine two blackbirds mating and hatching a canary? Say what? "Say, Ruby, can't you get Blondie to cool it on the tweet-tweet-tweet? I think we got problems in this neighborhood."

A crashing sound. Ruy bashed away at the bird with the broom. Ruy followed the bird into the living room. And, suddenly, Ruy was thinking of his childhood. A birthday party. He recalled a *piñata*—one of those paper-festooned ceramic crocks in the shapes of donkeys or parrots or stars that blindfolded children, at birthday parties, would swat at with a stick. The *piñata* was filled with candies and good things to eat and small gifts, and a boy was blindfolded, swinging at it. As a child the blindfold was placed over his eyes, he was spun around several times, handed the stick and then pointed in the direction of the *piñata* to swat at it and, hopefully, with one mighty swing, smash the ceramic pot—gaily decorated with colorful paper—sending its contents bursting through the air. Holding the broom in his hand, chasing the bird, Ruy remembered being blindfolded and then being spun around into laughter, unquenchable laughter. In total darkness he swung wildly at the *piñata,* at the blackbird. What gay happy times. Gone. Gone forever. Beyond the blindfold of age, he could see the entire thing. A mighty swing at the *piñata* sent its bright contents bursting from a ceramic parrot into a bright sun, and then raining out in a dozen directions. The *piñata* had been filled with candy of every description and small toys and packaged gifts. That had been such a lovely birthday party. His attractive mother had made tamales and everyone that he knew had come to give him lavish, expensive gifts: games, toys, clothes. It had all been so beautiful. The bird flew back into the room and perched on a windowsill. Ruy looked at the bird and sighed. The silly smile on Ruy's face completely unnerved the poor bird, Ralph. It quivered mightily and soiled the windowsill. Ruy's face suddenly hardened. The offensive act destroyed his childhood memories, his childhood fantasy, the gaily decorated *piñata*. A perfect birthday party.

Ruy screamed, and the bird began to pray to God for salvation. He said four Our Fathers and five Hail Marys. The bird's prayers were answered. Amapola walked into the house, swinging open the front door, leaving it open. The bird, spotting its chance for freedom, flew out of the house, out beyond the banana tree, thankful, sincerely thankful, exalting yet another day of freedom and life. And off it flew, up, up and away.

Ruy studied the effects of the evil omen. The bird had been a dark sign. One had but to look around at the damage left by the bird to realize that Ruy had been right. What a mess: broken lamps, smashed picture frames, a sad fern lying on its side, dirt spilling out of a broken flowerpot.

How fragile was life. How breakable its parts. A guy slams his fist into something and just like that, poof, it disappears, shatters to pieces. Things broke so easily. So what if a guy had a little bit of a temper, thought Ruy. Heck, it was good to let it out. You weren't supposed to keep it all bottled inside of you like the *gabachos* did. After all, look at them with their insanity and their ulcers and heart attacks and assassinations. It was bad for the liver or kidneys or something to keep the anxiety all locked up. But, *hijole,* nothing ever lasted. Ruy simply could not believe how poorly things were produced nowadays. Everything was so fragile and temporary.

Amapola screamed as she saw the destruction around her. It was the lamp, Amapola's little lamp, that was the last, the final straw. It was the lamp given to her by her brother,

Chava, her favorite brother, the one who was killed in Vietnam, part of that great mass of Hispanic cannon fodder now sacrificed regularly and patriotically in U.S. wars. That little cheap lamp, the one Chava had bought at Woolworth's. Amapola chose to dwell on the shattered pieces of the garish lamp, for in her mind, the pieces summarized Ruy's destructiveness, his savagery, and above all his insensitivity.

Amapola shook her head. Somewhere in the back of her mind, a little door closed, a valve was shut, a ringing telephone went unanswered. It was at that moment that Amapola vowed she would not speak to Ruy for as long as she lived.

# 11. The Hanky-panky

Hanky-panky may not make the world go round but it can give it a good spin. Hanky-panky makes it all worthwhile: the absurdity of it all, the silliness, the rude waiters. Without hanky-panky what would we be? Conservatives, curmudgeons afraid to parachute out of airplanes, go bungee jumping or eat jalapeño peppers. In other words, Republicans.

Those who engage in hanky-panky make good entrepreneurs, stock market brokers or kayakers, rock climbers and white-water rafters. They also make excellent lovers, particularly the fat ones. They aren't afraid of taking chances. They are not afraid. Hanky-panky practitioners are stimulated by adventure and danger—particularly when the woman's husband happens to be an irrational, hot-tempered, maniacal Mexican who is capable of exploding into a rage at a moment's notice and chasing some poor bird around his house destroying everything in his path.

If done correctly, hanky-panky can be as invigorating as a plunge into a cold mountain stream in May. Yes, it will be bracing at first but afterwards one can loll around on a warm rock bare-bottomed, cleansed, free, refreshed, smelling the tart fragrance of wild azaleas and a lover's sweet breath.

Hanky-panky is good for you. Don't try to moralize yourself out of it. You will only regret it later when you're looking at retirement property in Scottsdale, AZ, Fort Lauderdale, FL, or Ixtapa-Zihuatanejo.

"Guess, Dolores, guess, who is doing the hanky-panky?" asked Señorita Lucrecia. She was, of course, talking to her dear friend and scandal-mongering colleague, Señorita Dolores.

"Oh, tell me. Who?"

"This one you will not believe."

"Oh, please, for the love of God!" Señorita Lucrecia was being absolutely heartless with her dearest friend.

"Guess. Just guess. Who, in a million years, would you guess?"

"I give up, Lucrecia. Tell me."

"You will not believe this. It's . . . it's . . . I still cannot believe it . . ."

"Oh, God . . . Who? Please! You can be so cruel."

"Amapola."

"*¿Qué?*"

"Amapola."

Señorita Dolores's mouth went open with disbelief, revealing a set of ill-made dentures. "*¿Qué?*" There was a considerable pause. "Did you say Amapola."

"The same."

"Amapola Lopez?"

"*Sí.*"

"Ruy Lopez's wife?"

"That very one."

"*Ave María Purísima.* I do not believe it."

"Neither did I. I still do not believe it."

"Amapola? Ruy's wife?"

"The same."

"But she's so . . . so fat. So dark. She's not even pretty."

"It does not matter, dear. Love is blind."

"Who is her lover?"

"You are not going to believe it."

"Who?"

"You will die when I tell you."

"Please!"

"Pelon."

"Who?"

"Pelon."

"Pelon? The crybaby?"

"Him."

"*Santa María, Madre de Dios.* That poor man chain-smokes and always looks as though a sneeze would blow him away."

"That very one."

"How do you know? You are making this up."

"I am not. You know me better. I saw them together at Mission Dolores Park; up on the bridge that crosses the streetcar tracks near the statue of Miguel Hidalgo. They were walking away. You will not believe this. Holding hands. Can you believe that?"

"*Maldita sea . . .* Are you sure it was them?"

"I saw them with my own two eyes."

"Your eyes are not too good anymore, *querida.* Did you have your binoculars?"

"Of course, my new autofocus ones. And that is not all."

"There's more?"

"Yes. More. Before they parted they gave each other a long kiss."

"Where?"

"On the mouth."

"On the mouth?"

"Where else?"

"*Mira nomas. Aiii, Dios mío.* How can she stand to kiss him like that? He smokes like a chimney. Kissing him must be like kissing an ashtray."

"A *dirty* ashtray."

"*Aiii, qué cochinada.*"

"You must not breathe a single word of this to anyone."

"Of course not. What do you take me for, a *chismonera*, a tattletale?"

"No, no, of course not."


It took exactly twenty-six minutes for Amapola's affair with Pelon to begin circulating across the Mission District grapevine. After Señorita Lucrecia told Señorita Dolores—as she was duty-bound to do—Señorita Dolores told Señora Talavera; she, good-hearted soul that she was, told all of her cousins and nieces and nephews, who spread the message around more effectively than KCBS, the award-winning all-news radio station, and the front page of the Sunday edition of the *San Francisco Examiner.*

Little wonder men and women in love often go mad. One should try to be understanding. There they are one day singing a Broadway tune—"I've got a horse right here, his name is Paul Revere . . ."—painting the back fence, not a worry in their heads, a jingle in their pockets. And the next day there they are panting like summer dogs in the Sacramento—San Joaquin Valley sun, making fools of themselves, saying the most asinine things to their newfound sweethearts. And then later, love removed, they become tormented and delirious. What can you expect? The only logical thing to do is to go berserk. Try to be understanding. Give them a break. The next time you see a hysterical woman at a shopping mall involved in an irrational shopping and feeding frenzy, try to understand what could be going on. The next time you see a delirious young man carefully driving a caterpillar tractor across a row of cars parked in parallel don't simply dismiss him as an aberration or a loon. Ask yourself three things:

1. Is he about to drive over my car?

2. Will my insurance cover it? And, most important:

3. Could that shy, nice young man, that sweet-looking one with the angelic face methodically driving the tractor neatly over all of those Chevys and Fords, could he be the product of unrequited love? Aren't love and madness nothing but gospel-singing soul sisters? I'm talking to you. Answer the question. Don't look away from me when I'm talking to you!

For Amapola and Pelon it was madness, nothing less. Their passion; their lunacy, their hanky-panky. It was as if they would explode from it. The hand-holding. The hugging. The kissing. The and-so-forth and the and-so-on. They would swoon when they saw each other. They could stand in the middle of the street, not in the middle of the sidewalk, the middle of the street, totally aware of nothing but their own roiling passion, oblivious to everything but their own eyes and lips, their murmuring, their beating hearts. It was as if each word they uttered was meant to be etched with a laser in steel and then buried in a time capsule for 100,000 years.

"How is my little pigeon?" would produce sighs as tears would begin to well.

"My sweetheart."

"My darling."

A runaway truck rolling uncontrollably down Powell Street without brakes, its tires skidding on fog-moistened cable car tracks, its horn blaring, the driver's face ashen with fear, would not faze them. Nor would flood nor earthquake, nor the acrid smell of fresh paint nor the unbearable and detestable sound of fingernails being trimmed with a nail clipper. Nothing could touch them but their own searing lunacy.

"Oh, honey."

"Oh, baby."

For some perverse reason, which only the two of them found amusing, they began to call each other "shit" and "piss."

"Where are you, my sweet little piece of warm shit?" Pelon would ask coyly, and Amapola would sing out, "I'm over here, my little cup of warm baby piss."

These two words, and their variations, took on an intense personal significance. In a department store, one would yell out, "Shitter!" and the other would yell back, to everyone's annoyance, "Yes, pisser?"

"Shitter!"

"Pisser!"

"Shitter!"

"Pisser!"

And they would fly toward each other like two heat-seeking missiles and tumble into each other's arms in an ecstatic, swooning embrace. Right there. In the middle of the discount basement.

"Oh, my shitter," "Oh, my pisser," they would coo as if reciting Shakespearian sonnets.

Words cannot describe the loathing felt by people listening to these scatological mating calls.

As can be imagined, the affair produced an unstoppable deluge of tears from the eyes of Pelon.

At Sunday mass it seemed as if the entire parish was waiting anxiously for the appearance of the cuckolded Ruy and the adulterous Amapola. The midget, Eufemio Galian, kept turning, craning his neck whenever anyone entered the church. The tension was unbearable. Señorita Dolores and Señorita Lucrecia could hardly stand the emotional strain which was mercifully relieved by the ringing of the sanctuary bell signaling the start of the ten o'clock mass.

*"Ed introibo ad altare Dei."*

Bunny García scraped her painted fingernails across the mesh of a stockinged thigh creating a sandpaper sound. She did it once, twice, a third time. Manny Caballos could hardly help noticing. Perhaps Bunny had contracted some rare skin disease, he thought; something like poison oak. But, of course, it couldn't be poison oak. About the only place one could possibly find poison oak in the Mission District of San Francisco would be in some kind of poison oak museum—if someone were stupid enough to want to waste his time starting up such a ridiculous thing.

Caballos exhaled, shook his head. And yet, you never knew with these crazy *gringos.* He looked up at the altar. Oh, God, don't even think of it. Just the thing that some bureaucratic *pendejo* in Washington, D.C., might think would be important for the San Francisco "Hispanic Community." Caballos allowed the entire thought to play itself out in his mind. He gave the idea full rein:

Yes, he could see it all. Some bleeding Washington bureaucrat might think that a poison oak program might be just the thing to educate the poor, unfortunate Hispanics of the Mission District, part of a nature enrichment program. Some wise-guy consultant would make a proposal to the Department of Education or the Department of Health and Human Services for a community outreach program based on poison oak. The plan would be passed and some bald, bearded, pot-bellied retread hippie from the sixties with a degree in poison oak from U.C. Berkeley would be picked to run the program. The Berkeley retread hippie, wearing Mexican sandals whose soles consisted of pieces of automobile tires, would develop an expensive slide show which he would take around to various schools and community centers and present it along with a number of poison oak songs which he would sing, accompanying himself on a water-stained guitar. He wouldn't bathe because he would assume that Hispanics never took baths and because he wanted to "reach out to those people. Let them know that I am one of them."

An office would be set up in the Mission District on either Sixteenth or Twenty-fourth Street. On opening day, there would be speeches from the politicians plus a high school band and young dancers wearing colorful ethnic costumes. A ribbon would be cut by the Mayor, and the poison oak community office would be officially dedicated. First the desks and chairs and then the photocopy machine, the telephone lines, the fax machines and the computers. People would be hired. The balding Berkeley retread hippie with the potbelly would insist that "you've simply got to get into the synergistic value of the poison oak experience in order to understand the message that we must communicate to our brown brothers. I hear ya." In English, that meant that all potential employees were to roll around in poison oak and become horribly sick from it for a month before they could be hired. Special "field experience" trips would be arranged into the hills south of San Francisco and prospective employees would be asked to strip down to their underwear and then roll across bushes of poison oak. The practice would continue until some disgruntled employee, who hated bald, retread hippies, would complain to the Department of Labor that the practice constituted sexual harassment. "One should not be forced to strip down to one's skivvies in order to get a job." Jesse Jackson would appear at a Civic Center rally opposing the hiring practice. ("This affects *all* of my minorities: the blacks, the browns, the reds, the yellows, the fuchsia, the lavender and the teal. This affects all of my *people*.") The hiring practice would be discontinued and Jackson would announce that he would not run for President.

And all the while, Mission District Hispanics would be wondering:

"What in the fuck are these crazy *gringos* up to now? What will they come up with next? A Hispanic *caca* museum? 'Good, morning, *Caca*. How may I direct your call?' "

Caballos stared at a Crucifixion scene in his prayer book. He shook his head. Best not to even think about it. And yet nothing, nothing, was totally out of the question; nothing could be ruled out with the crazy bureaucratic *gringos*.

Bunny García scraped her fingernails over the mesh of her stockinged thigh once again. What she was scratching was a monkey bite administered passionately the night before by one of her most ardent customers, the implacable Judge Abelardo Quintana. *"Aiii,* Abe, take it easy. You are such a sensuous man. Try not to leave any marks."

And then in the middle of Father *In*Clemente's sermon —his topic that Sunday morning was "Adultery and the Sins of the Flesh"—they arrived. Ruy and Amapola finally made their appearance at the ten o'clock mass at 10:32 A.M. When they appeared, pairs of heads could be seen bobbing together like corks in water as the cuckolded Ruy and the adulterous Amapola made their way into a church pew. Ruy was oblivious to the din they created. The stir mortified Amapola, who was sure everyone knew, which indeed they did.

Father *In*Clemente seemed to be firing his words directly at Amapola: "carnal knowledge," "lasciviousness," "lust," "prurience," "sodomy," "lecherousness," "bestiality," "fornication." With every pronouncement, Father *In*Clemente's voice got louder. He was in his element. As always, he was in his cups. Amapola kept her head bowed, shielding herself from Father *In*Clemente's excoriating words. And Ruy's thoughts, as usual, drifted off, away, this time to Winifred Lampson Birdwell and her milk-white hands with their long, slender fingers. Her hands could appear so white, so small, grasping his dark, erect penis. The powerful words spoken by Father *In*Clemente could hardly describe the small-chef's-salad-with-Thousand-Island-dressing affair he was having with her. It was like someone burping into a bouquet of pussy willows; it could hardly be called sin. Besides, what the hell did *In*Clemente know about nooky anyway? Why didn't he stick to something he knew something about? Booze.

"Thus are the words of this Sunday's Gospel," chanted Father *In*Clemente.

Amen and thank God.

# 12. Ruy's Dilemma

On Monday Ruy Lopez caught diarrhea.

In the midst of his profound confusion, a growling intestine snapped him out of a daydream of butterflies. Even his stomach was beginning to betray him, he thought. It had to be the result of tension, or that chronic Mexican disorder, *nervios*. Perhaps he should take the classic Mexican cure-all: a laxative or an enema. To be truthful, some of the growling *was* nerves, but most of it was caused by a luncheon dish prepared for him that day by his mistress, Winifred Lampson Birdwell: a thick sausage in a rich, white cream sauce served on a bed of wild rice.

"This dish reminds me of our relationship, Roo-Eez, baby," Winifred whispered, "particularly the thick Andouille sausage," she added, rubbing her ankle against Ruy's hairy thigh.

The sauce contained too much butter, too much heavy cream. It disagreed with him even though he had restrained himself and taken only thirds. Ruy could hardly stand the pain in his stomach and had to leave Winifred's warm bed.

"Tummy wanna go 'ouchie,' Roo-Eez, baby?"

"Tummy wanna go 'boom-boom,' Winnie," said Ruy. "May I be excused?"

"Oh, Roo-Eez, baby."

A disappointed Winifred waved at Ruy as he dashed away from her Pacific Heights home. Ruy drove hurriedly,

parked his pickup truck and dashed into his house past a
slumbering Lulusa the dog and a yawning Molly the cat.

"Oh-oh," said Molly.

Lulusa snapped awake. "What's the matter?"

"Guess who just walked in?"

"You're kidding."

"Nope. It's Himself, his nibs."

"Ooooh, shee-eet. It's going to hit the fan around here."

"This should be good."

"I don't know about you, Molly, but I'm hightailing it
the hell out of here."

"I'm right behind you."

For Ruy the matter was getting desperate. As he dashed
through the house on his way to the bathroom, he could hear
two voices.

"Oh, my shitter!"

"Oh, my pisser!"

What the hell was that? On his way down the hallway,
Ruy glanced into his bedroom to see his wife in bed with
Pelon. Her naked brown rump was up in the air and Pelon
was spraying whipped cream across it from a pressurized can
creating a happy face with a wide stupid smile.

"Oh, my shitter!"

"Oh, my pisser!"

Ruy rushed into the bathroom, dropped his pants and
baggy shorts and sat down. This had turned out to be an
incredible emergency. He was in lamentable pain.

He took a deep breath. No, it was much too ridiculous,
too silly to even contemplate. He had only imagined it: Pelon
drawing a happy face on his wife's bare bottom with whipped

cream while they called each other "shitter" and "pisser." No, no, it was simply too much. Would this incredible dream, this nightmare, never end? Now even his stomach and his mind—his eyes and ears—were rebelling against him. But then there it was. Beneath the shuffling confusion in the bedroom, he could hear Pelon sniffing gently. This was no dream. Pelon was going to cry. Oh, my God. Pelon was fooling around with his own wife, Amapola? ·

Pelon cleared his throat. "I can explain to you everything, and I must, *carnal,*" said Pelon bravely. "We were going to tell you." Ruy groaned, closed his eyes. He couldn't believe it. He was in agony. What was there to explain? Amapola was in bed with Pelon, who had sprayed whipped cream on her bottom. The thought of whipped cream nauseated Ruy. He rubbed his mouth.

"This is not what it appears to be," said Amapola, breaking her vow of eternal silence. She had not spoken to him in several days.

If only his guts weren't killing him. If only he weren't sitting on the johnny taking a profound dump, he might even enjoy Amapola's explanation. How unfair it can all be sometimes. Ruy had always imagined how he would react to this kind of scene: outrage, screaming, brutality, tears, death. A terrific Mexican scene: *The Revenge of the Cuckolded Husband,* starring Ruy and Amapola Lopez. He had savored the moment when, love-alienated, he could kill his wife's lover. Sheer poetry. He had seen it in countless dramas. But instead, there he was sitting on the johnny, wrenching his guts out, his stomach in excruciating pain.

In the poetic Mexican scenario, one shot would dispatch

the wife's lover to the hereafter. How beautifully true it would be. How noble, how genuine, how Mexican, how ridiculous. But in reality, there was sad Pelon in his bedroom sobbing and Ruy was there in the bathroom squatting on the privy being tortured by his stomach. Life could be so unfair. It doesn't even allow us the chance to play out the scenarios in our most heartfelt fantasies when the opportunity appears. He hardly had the strength or the will for outrage now. He simply wanted his stomach to get well and to find his mystery woman, who was driving him nuts. Ruy studied the cleanliness of his bathroom floor. No wonder the sheets had been changed with such regularity.

Pelon's sobs got louder. Ruy muttered, "That's all right, Pelon. *Mira,* don't cry, these things happen."

All he could think of was his mother's lifesaving expression, *"Sea por Dios."* Ruy smiled. What could he possibly do? What could he possibly say that wouldn't compound the stupidity of this incredible farce? Why did everything have to be so complicated? Life could be such a confusing mess. A genuine stupidity, a *tarugada.*

Pelon's sobs got louder. "I'm sorry, man . . . I . . . I . . ." He groped for the exact words. He wanted to be sincere. "I didn't mean to fuck Amapola. I don't know what's the matter with me, *ese.* I don't know what came over me; what . . ." Pelon was practically screaming out his sorrow. Before he could finish his sentence, a fresh round of grief and tears erupted.

"Oh, man, take it easy. *¿Sabes?*"

Pelon poured out a fresh torrent of tears. "Why don't you just kill me, *carnal,*" pleaded Pelon. "Let me have it. Right now! Make it quick. I deserve it."

Ruy grimaced. Knots were tightening across both his small and large intestines. He unrolled approximately eighteen yards of toilet paper.

"Don't be stupid. Look, Pelon, why don't you just leave. ¿*Sabes?*" Ruy's guts groaned. They pronounced the very sadness in his soul.

The following day, Ruy found a note in Amapola's stumpy handwriting:

Dear Husband:

I am leaving you. You always want what you cannot have, because most of the time you do not know what you want. You live in a dream. Nothing is real for you. You drink too much and you cannot control your temper. You do not make love to me like a man. I think you have been around too many *maricones*. When you catch me with another man you do not beat him up even though he is smaller than you, and you do not beat me up. You are not a man. You are a coward. I have found true love with Pelon. He smokes too much but he has promised to quit for my love. He is more of a man than you are. He cries but that is because he is sensitive and has feelings, which you do not have. I know you are fooling around with another woman. I have read her notes, the ones that she writes on that stinking paper. You may be her *"Hombre Hermoso"* but you are no longer mine. Like it says in that old Frank Sinatra song, "It was just one of those things. A trip to the moon on gossamer wings," et cetera. I will never return. Good-bye forever. *Adiós.*

Your ex-wife,
Amapola

P.S.: Do not forget to feed Lulusa and Molly.

In that day's mail there arrived another one of those perfectly crafted notes that smelled of vanilla that always began, *"Mi Hombre Hermoso."*

"Things cannot possibly get any worse," said Ruy.

# 13. The Prince of Darkness

When Delfina decided to make a pact with the Devil, she didn't know where to start. She could find no reference books or how-to manuals. To begin with, she was a bit shy about approaching him, the Prince of Darkness, as Father *In-Clemente* always called him. She pondered her dilemma. She even consulted with her *gatito*.

"Benjie, how do you think I should reach the Devil? To God you pray directly and never get your prayers answered. But to the Devil? How do you reach him?"

Benjie licked his paw and then his face.

"I bet my *ratero* nephew, Conde Pacheco, would know."

Benjie hissed at the sound of the name. Even dogs and cats knew that Conde Pacheco was immoral. Conde had once sold Delfina a jogging watch that turned out to be stolen and a television set that worked for two days and then blew up.

"Can you imagine doing that to your own *tía?* Maybe I could ask that *sinvergüenza,* that rat nephew of mine, how he talks to the Devil."

Delfina pondered her dilemma. If she contacted Conde he would probably try to sell her a broken washing machine or a refrigerator that kept everything hot.

"But how can I ask him to help me, Benjie? How?" Benjie stretched, digging his claws into the sofa. "What do I do; say, 'Excuse me, Conde, you big *ratón,* but could you please tell me how you communicate with your good friend Satan?'" Benjie yawned.

Delfina thought it over. If Conde helped her he would probably end up blackmailing her or, at the very least, charging her a bundle. That's the way things always worked out. You always had to pay a bundle for everything with an arm or a leg through the nose.

But how could *she* reach the Devil? To God you prayed to Him on your knees with your clothes on. Maybe to reach the Devil you sat back in your easy chair in a teddy or negligee in the dark and played dirty rock and roll music. ("C'm on, mama, gimme some.") She wondered if the Devil spoke English or Spanish. Probably English, she figured. The Spanish proverb went: "To speak to a woman about love you must speak to her in French, but to speak to God you must speak to Him in Spanish." The obvious extension to that one, thought Delfina, would be, ". . . and to speak to the Devil you must speak to him in English." It was worth a try. What did she have to lose but her immortal soul?

Delfina dimmed all of the lights in her small Mission District home. The last thing she wanted was someone like Señorita Lucrecia or Señorita Dolores to see her. She put on a pair of flannel pajamas and bathrobe and put out the cat. She did not want Benjie to be a witness to the terrible, evil act she was about to commit. When Benjie was gone she closed the door and then produced a picture of St. Michael the Archangel who was flying through the air holding a golden sword in one hand and the scales of justice in the other. She folded the picture to show only the bottom part, an image of a dark, cowering Satan about to be chopped into little pieces by Michael's sword. She placed the folded picture on a chair next to a red votive candle. Delfina propped up two pillows and then lay back on the living room sofa.

"Dear Devil, you do not know me from Adam. I have always tried to avoid you like sin itself. I know you are down there in . . ." She shuddered. Even though she wanted to reach him she was unwilling to even think of the name of the Devil's residence. She started over.

"Dear Devil, you do not know me from Adam, but I was wondering if I could ask you a little favor. Here is the situation. I am tired of praying all of the time for things I never get. I am tired of asking for mercy for sins I do not commit. People are always blaming me. On the TV everyone blames me for everything. They blame me for creating holes in the sky and warming up the earth. They blame me for killing the forests and for getting the rivers and the oceans dirty and for killing little birds and seals and whales and elephants in Africa. *¡Ya que!* I've never even been to Africa. How could I kill something I've only seen on the TV? Father *In*Clemente is always accusing me of sins I do not commit. He is always making me feel bad about things I can't even do anymore. He makes me feel bad just for living. I am getting tired. My bunions are hurting me and I want to play before I go. I want to go to parties. I want to have fun.

"Look, Devil, I am no longer a little girl. I have been praying to God all my life for things that I have never received. I am getting tired of this for it is nothing but *caca*. For all of my praying I have received nothing but two knees with calluses and plenty of scolding from Father *In*Clemente, who is seldom ever sober. Oh sure, I received a little sewing machine from my sister. But I really did not want it. After sewing at the factory all my life I do not ever want to sew again. Besides, it was a cheap machine, a piece of chit. I do not often use this kind of language but I am told you use this kind of language all the time and prefer it to the regular kind. Anyway, there was also Panchito, my husband; well, not really my husband since we were never married. He was my common in-law husband. *¿Sabes?* He was fat and used to get drunk and beat me up, but that was O.K. At least I was not lonely. Now here I am alone, a *viuda,* a widow. Since the death of Panchito I had been praying to God for a nice older man to keep me company. He did not have to be a gentleman or very good looking. *¡Ya que!* At my age I am not choosy.

Delfina smiled, exposing a row of uneven teeth. She shook her head and continued her blasphemous prayer. "Now, Devil, I know I am too old to have another man so I am not going to even ask you for one. That would be like asking for the impossible, even from you. What I want is a car. I can still drive a car. I want to see my sister, Chencha, in Fresno more often; before either of us starts to die. We had a car until Panchito smashed it into the tree and had to be hospitalized. Panchito, not the tree. The hospital took all our money. Even the guy that owned the tree wanted to sue me for his stinking tree until he found out Panchito had suffered a heart attack when he saw the hospital bill. Panchito died soon after that. Losing the car and getting the bill killed him. That and all the tequila he had to drink to forget the car and the hospital bill.

"It would be nice to have a car, Devil, and not have to use the bus or the BART, which is so expensive. Try going to

Fresno without a car. Forget it. A new car would be nice, Devil. A little *Foringo* or a *Cheeby* would be fine." Delfina remembered that, in negotiating, one starts at the top, not the bottom. "I want *Cadiyác,* Devil. I want to drive a new *Cadiyác* with a little green pine tree deodorizer board hanging from the mirror making everything smell nice. A pretty *Cadiyác* would be best of all. I was only kidding about the *Foringo* or the *Cheeby.*" Delfina made her closing argument. "And I do not care if you take me with you to Hell for all Eternity. That will be better than going to Heaven and being bored by people like Father *In*Clemente and Señorita Dolores and Señorita Lucrecia. O.K.? I am serious. Look, I am ready to cut a deal with you, Devil. Honest to God."

That night, she drove a car at 980 miles per hour through the gates of Hell, only to snap awake suddenly. *"Aiii, it was only a dream. It seemed so real."*

# 14. The Discovery

After uttering his dying words, "Darling, you're insatiable," he smiled, closed his eyes and went out with the ebb, leaving Winifred Lampson Birdwell a disorder of staggering proportions.

"Oh, Roo-Eez, baby, I simply cannot tell you what an absolutely botched mess that SOB has created by dying." The SOB Winifred referred to was her late husband, the one who had gone to Brazil on a business trip and had never returned; the one who had decided to stay there after meeting the alluring twenty-one-year-old woman with cinnamon skin who smelled of apples.

"How did he die?" asked Ruy.

"He fucked his brains out," responded Winifred. When she explained that the woman her husband had met had turned out to be a sex maniac and that he had died by overindulging in sex, Ruy whimpered like a kicked puppy. His eyes glazed over as he pondered the dearly departed, for as far as Ruy was concerned that was the noblest way for a man to die. It was also one of his dearest fantasies: to die smiling, exhausted, in a state of total dissipation, *The Last Great Temptation and Proud Erection of Ruy Lopez Mondragon.*

"Roo-Eez, are you all right, baby?" asked Winifred.

"Sha-sha . . . Sure . . . sugar."

"You, of course, know what this means, don't you, Roo-Eez, bay-bee?" Ruy, of course, did *not* know. "It means I'll have to go down to Brazil to straighten out that god-awful mess he's left. I'll have to do something about his body and belongings and my lawyer tells me he purchased some property down there in her name." Winnie reached over, took Ruy's hand and gave him a soulful stare which gave Ruy a close-up look at the crow's-feet around her eyes and the wrinkles at her neck. "It also means we'll be apart for a while." Ruy couldn't decide what taking a break from Winifred would mean. Sex with her had become so bland and routine as to become meaningless. The same egg salad on white bread with mayonnaise once a week. "I'm going to miss you, Roo-Eez."

He felt obliged to say something. He parroted back her statement. "I'm going to miss you too, Winnie." He hoped that the next thing he would say could sound sincere. "What am I going to do without you, Winnie?"

"Oh, that's terribly sweet," said Winnie. "You Lah-tee-nos can be *so* sentimental." Winifred stretched and began rubbing Ruy's chest. His attempt at sincerity had been swallowed.

When Winifred departed Ruy felt relieved. He could breathe easily. There would be no elaborate tea ceremonies for a while; no lemon cupcake sex with Guy Lombardo music in the background. Today Ruy would simply tend to Winifred's garden. It was much too hot to do anything fatiguing. It was only 10:30 A.M. and he was already perspiring *a la gota gorda*.

Ruy assessed the need to trim Mrs. Birdwell's tall hedges which surrounded a swimming pool. The sides were O.K. but sometimes the tops—which could be seen from the second-story windows in the house—could be scraggly. He climbed a ladder to look at the tops of the hedges. He assessed them carefully. They could wait another week. What the heck. And then he peered below at something by the swimming pool. Ruy was dumbstruck. His eyes widened. What he saw was so phenomenal, so stunning, that he almost fell off of the ladder.

There before him was a wondrous sight: Mrs. Birdwell's spectacular daughter, Alexis, nude, sunning herself by the pool. Her body was covered with oil and her skin glistened. She lay on her back, covering her eyes with her right arm, her left leg crossing her right. And then she turned over slowly, carefully, revealing her backside before lying on her stomach. Ruy's vision intensified, tilted and then began to sway. Here was Ruy's perfect, everlasting dream: a flawless young body triumphant and golden in the morning sun. Ruy could not breathe. He began to tremble. He descended carefully, sliding his wet palms along the sides of the ladder. When he was safely off the ladder he knelt on the wet earth and crossed himself with his right hand—from forehead to stomach, from left shoulder to right—bowed his head, folded his hands and recited that lovely masterpiece: the prayer of St. Francis:

"Lord, make me an instrument of Your peace,
  Where there is hatred, let me sow love;
  Where there is injury, pardon . . ."

It was as if Ruy had been allowed to witness a supernal vision. He walked away. He could feel himself throbbing. He slipped into his truck, let it coast silently down the driveway before starting it and driving off. Alexis's unimaginable beauty was matched by an astonishing, perfect body. Ruy swallowed. His throat felt dry. He offered a silent prayer to all of the Holy Saints in Heaven, for he was grateful, sincerely grateful, for what he had just witnessed.

It was a difficult day for Ruy. The heat of the day matched the fervor of his thoughts. Every angle became Alexis's arms, Alexis's legs; every curve Alexis's proud, shimmering, tanned bottom.

It was almost unfair. He felt so helpless, so trapped in his own cravings. The slightest hint would force a vision of a honeyed body, arms, legs, a slow turning and then, only then, those two perfect golden roundnesses.

That night Ruy perspired. The night brought no relief. He couldn't sleep, it was simply too hot. There were too many concerns. Amapola had left him for that silly Pelon, who smoked those terrible cigars and cried like a baby. Lulusa, his dog, was being haughty to him. Molly the cat was picking up Lulusa's cues. She too was being nasty and distant. The property for one of the largest yards on his gardening route was being sold and he feared he would lose that income. And now his sister, Esmeralda, was calling him nightly with sad complaints about her new husband, Judge Abelardo Quintana.

"He doesn't love me. He doesn't want to do *anything*. He does not even want to make love to me anymore. We never go out. He hates to dance. He says it hurts his feet. Oh, Ruy, I thought I would be so happy. Instead I am so miserable. I am the most miserable person on this earth . . ."

But nothing distressed Ruy more than that day's apparition, that dream which taunted him, which followed him everywhere, which was just beneath the surface of everything he attempted. And it would play itself out in his mind once again, for the one thousandth time: Alexis's body, the angles of her arms and legs, to her backside and then her bottom: two perfect curves glistening defiantly in the morning sun. And then, just below that, almost as distant as a remembered echo or the wheezing of midnight surf, he could hear the words *"Mi hombre hermoso."*

Life could be so complicated, so terribly unfair. Not to mention the heat, the unrelenting heat.

It was all too much. Ruy dressed himself and got into his truck. When he turned on the truck's air-conditioning a puff of dust emerged from the vents along with grass clippings and bits of leaves. *Hijo,* he hadn't used the air conditioner in a long time. He drove aimlessly, distractedly. The cool air felt good on his face. That was better. And then he remembered his ladder. He had left his ladder next to the hedges overlooking Mrs. Birdwell's pool. He would retrieve it. That's what he would do, retrieve his ladder, perform something useful, something purposeful on this long and harrowing night.

He drove to the Birdwell house, which was totally dark. He would be careful, remove the ladder and then slip away silently as he had done earlier.

When Ruy entered the back yard he could hear the burbling of the swimming pool's filtration system. It was so warm. A dip in the swimming pool would be nice. Yes. He would do it. In that total darkness he would slip silently into the water and cool off. He removed his clothes, wiped the perspiration from his face with his shirt and moved toward a corner of the pool where he reached out to touch the metal of a ladder railing. He turned, edged his way down the ladder and entered the water carefully without making a sound until his entire naked body was floating like a contented, fat manatee. He moved slowly in the water without splashing. He was cool and comfortable for the very first time that day. He sighed.

And then there it was again, that persistent remembrance, the smell of vanilla, the maze of hair. Two arms embraced him in the water.

*"Mi hombre hermoso,"* whispered in perfect Spanish, and then an anxious mouth devouring his lips. The realization. The smell of vanilla. The slim waist, the hair. Ruy was dazed.

"Alexis!"

This can't be real, thought Ruy. It can't be possible. She was too beautiful, too refined, too young. He was too plain, too vulgar. This was only another false dream from which he would soon emerge. A trick. Reality would soon overpower this dream and serve up the usual main course of War, Famine, Pestilence and Death; and side dishes of Racism, Poverty and Bills. And for dessert: the Flu, Surly Waiters, Dental Hygiene and, the worst calamity of all, Baldness.

But, no, this was real: the fragrance of vanilla, the long hair and she was there in the water with him, forming little circles in his ear with the tip of her tongue. Ruy could almost cry. Alexis had her arms and legs around him there in the water, by the shallow end of the pool. She was embracing him totally and she was nude.

*"Mi hombre hermoso,"* she kept repeating. And Ruy could feel the fine stirrings of a gallant, wondrous erection as a burble from the pool filtration system seemed to applaud and belch its approval.

And in a short while, they were out of the water and in her room and she was touching him, offering herself to him completely, whispering, *"Mi hombre hermoso,"* as she lowered herself over him, kissing him tenderly, guiding his erection into her own warmth. Ruy smiled. And then a powerful emotion swept over him. It was so overwhelming he almost cried as he offered a silent prayer. "Thank you, God. I thought for sure I was turning into a little *maricón*."

And from some aromatic wilderness, Alexis was there stalking him, surrounding him with the fragrance of vanilla, creating small circles on his skin with her fingertips, touching him, caressing him and he was glad. Now she was over him and he was inside of her and her hair was touching his chest and there was a tightening and a low moan. And then he was very deep inside of her, wrapped in a vanilla cocoon and her words were there to tease him, to taunt him once again.

*"Mi hombre hermoso."*

Never had the Spanish language sounded more beautiful. She had learned her flawless Castillian Spanish at the University of Salamanca. *"Mi hombre hermoso,"* she repeated, and it followed him even into his dreams of spectacular phantoms.

*"Te va gustar esto,"* said Alexis, and Ruy was pleased by the sound of her voice, her perfect Spanish.

On a starry night, Ruy could hear the mysterious sound of an owl *hoot-hoot-hooting*. Was this yet another dream from which he would soon be roused? Alexis was pressed against him and her body felt natural and right and his hand was touching something familiar and yet strange, a seed, a hard raisin between his fingertips, Alexis's nipple, as her mouth pressed against his. And yet another dream began to unfold. He heard the sigh of the owl. The superstitious Señora Talavera had once told him that a hooting owl was a sign of good fortune. And indeed it was. He never wanted this to end. As up somewhere, in Ruy's memory, the owl hooted approvingly. "I condone this, Ruy," said the owl. "A hoot to you for good luck and good fortune. She's a real knockout. *Hoot-hoot-hoot.*"

He was entangled in Alexis's long black hair, a web at his face; her soft hair was like a fine meshed net. Now her hair seemed to be windblown as it swept over his face. He didn't care. It was enough that it was brushing his face, sweeping over his warm eyelids, was touching his lips, his cheeks, his eyes and nose.

"*Aiii,* Alexis," Ruy whispered.

It was all too good and, therefore, it would never last. And he knew it. He knew that at any moment it could all end, it would all be gone, disappear forever. The dream was too perfect. It would soon be a memory. Nothing more. There could be no other way. The bright star would burn out, explode into millions of pieces and rain down on him, and then everything would return to its previous darkness, tedium, melancholy and isolation. The dance would be over, the play finished, the meal consumed. How could there ever be anything else? But for now, there was this, only this, and this alone. For now, this was all he ever wanted, even if it wouldn't last.

And then, from a dream of spice-filled barges floating slowly down a warm river past bright clusters of aromatic tropical flowers, there came a sensation of spinning, of circling, and he was falling, dropping straight down, only to loop out of his fall and then glide away pleasantly. Ruy emerged slowly from his dream. An expanding circle was being drawn on his stomach; a continuous series of spirals. Something was touching his fat, bare stomach and he awoke to see Alexis, her black hair nearly covering her green eyes.

She was smiling at him, rubbing her index finger around his belly button, and Ruy stretched like a sleek, contented cat. On that perfect morning, he felt boundless and strong as her leg rubbed against his thigh. At that very moment Ruy once again became all-powerful and invincible: immortal.

That day, in a supermarket, Ruy saw a ravishing woman. She was a striking beauty and she gave Ruy a perfect gift: a wonderful smile, and for the rest of the day Ruy was triumphant, for he had been touched by gods and goddesses and Alexis's firm breasts. Alexis's sex and aromas, still clinging to his lips, brought him great joy and another cascade of recollection.

What was to follow was the most lyrical period of Ruy's life, for is there anything sweeter than the process of making our own fresh discoveries of another person? It was a period of supreme Mexican elation. Ruy was thankful for everything he saw. Every sight was a joy. Each breath brought it all back: the sweetness of cinnamon and vanilla and, of course, nooky. His happiness was all-encompassing and he wanted to reach out and hug the world, the stars and the moon. Everything moved gently and carefully in exquisite dance patterns of superb order and grace. Everything finally made such perfect sense. He looked at Lulusa, his beagle-mix dog, as she urinated on a leaf and, somehow, that contemptible act took on the most poignant degree of cosmic order. "Of course," whispered Ruy. "We are one." Ruy's bliss was boundless and, needless to say, excessive. He knelt down in his back yard beneath the branches of his sycamore tree to give thanks to Almighty God for all the wonders of Creation and for His invention of nooky. Lulusa, wondering what the hell her crazy master was up to now, went over to a kneeling Ruy and sniffed at his shoes. Upon seeing the dog, Ruy was filled with an additional burst of elation. He reached over, took the dog in his arms and began to hug it mercilessly, rolling over on the ground with the dog until finally, the poor animal, close to suffocating from Ruy's embrace and the weight of his body, barked desperately and bit Ruy on the thigh before running off.

"Ungrateful, goddamn dog," screamed Ruy, massaging the spot on his thigh bitten by Lulusa. To think that only a few hours earlier that same spot had been licked deliciously and kissed tenderly by Alexis. There you are, now. What can we really say? Kiss today, bite tomorrow.

# La Lunita Restaurant

Lopez for Supervisor's unofficial campaign headquarters.

# 15. Politics

A row of *piñatas* hung from the ceiling stretching from the entrance of the restaurant to a corner where two boys were playing a video arcade game. On a television set an Argentinian soccer match competed for loudness with a jukebox playing an accordion-backed Mexican *"norteña"* song which spoke of love, betrayal and death.

The tables were set with paper place mats and chrome napkin containers. A triangular sign at each table advertised Tecate beer. Manny Caballos shook hands with Victor Lopez as they sat down to lunch at La Lunita.

As usual, Caballos came right to the point.

"I want you to run against Meester for Supervisor."

Victor laughed.

"Run against Meester, von Meisterding? He's too solid. He has money. Besides, I don't have any experience."

"You're young but not inexperienced. You're a commissioner . . ."

Victor smiled. "Commissioner? *¿Qué va?* Park and Recreation. I want a park for the Mission District. That's not experience."

"Yes, it is. Shows your concern for the District. You have more experience than when Meester got elected. You started the Mexican-American Judicial Fund and Educational Affiliation. You know how to reach the corporate people . . ."

"We're backed by *some* corporations. The thing's just getting started."

"What *is* the purpose of your group?"

"We're a corporate-backed fund aimed at legally forcing ethnic gerrymandering."

"I'm not sure what that means but it sounds good. I do know that your group is bringing about effective change."

"*Gracias,* Señor Caballos. It's a small drop of water."

"Yeah, but it works. Look, I want you to run. You're married. You have a lovely family, you're a good-looking guy, you look nice on TV and you make a good bullshit speech. That's called a politician. Besides, what the hell are you waiting for? Everyone looks to you for leadership. Besides, it's wrong not to have a Hispanic on the Board of Supervisors."

"But why me?"

"You're young. You're clean. You haven't been corrupted." Manny Caballos paused for effect. "Yet." Victor laughed. "We need a Hispanic running for office."

"What about Sergio Barajas? He's running for Mayor. He's Mexican. And Belmonte just got appointed Supervisor. He's running for reelection."

"*¡Madre Santísima!* Sergio Barajas is a *payaso,* a clown, and you know that. All he's after is publicity for his theaters. He will do anything for publicity. No one really takes him seriously. As for Chacon Belmonte, nice guy but there's nothing there," said Caballos, tapping his forehead. "He's a safe political appointment, following Murphy's death. He'll vote any way the Mayor wants him to. And he's doing everything he can to get himself defeated in November. Every time he opens his mouth he says something embarrassing. Besides, how can Belmonte get reelected? Even the Anglo liberals think he's stupid, and that's bad. He can't even get the bleeders. It's over before it begins. His appointment was a political trick. Pacify the Hispanics by appointing a self-destructive moron, put him up for an election he can't possibly win, and then support his opponent. It's all stacked. I'm talking about a Hispanic from *La Michon*." And then Caballos pronounced each of his words carefully. "We need a Mission District Hispanic on the Board of Supervisors. That could be you."

"I don't know that I'm the one. My organization is just getting started; so is my law practice."

"Public office will give both your organization and your law practice greater exposure. Public office is giving Belmonte exposure and Barajas the Clown publicity."

"I can't afford to run for office."

Caballos shook his head, smiled. "Money can be raised. Deals can be struck. Listen, I'm serious. Tony Bradlee will be joining us here in just a few minutes."

"Bradlee? The professional campaign guy for the Democrats?"

"Yes."

"Bradlee? He used to run big statewide campaigns."

"Used to. He could run your campaign if you agreed."

"But why?"

"He needs the money. Three ex-wives all want alimony, kids need child support."

"Bradlee? Running a Mission District campaign? Jesus! The guy's a legend. What happened to him?"

"Even big shots run into problems. Legends have to eat, so do their ex-wives. Look, there he is now. Do me a favor, O.K.? Just be quiet and listen. O.K.? Do me a favor."

"Well . . ."

Bradlee appeared, shook hands. "I hope you don't mind, but I've asked Sergio Barajas to join us."

Caballos looked at Victor, who looked at Bradlee. Bradlee appeared dissipated and very tired, the victim of thirty years of campaigning. Drink had etched its mark on his face, and nicotine had stained his fingers. His suit, which reeked of tobacco, needed cleaning and pressing. Victor was almost embarrassed. He had studied some of Anthony Bradlee's classic campaigns in political science courses at the university. Major propositions that had brought profound changes to California, initiatives, candidates. It seemed sad to Victor that the great Anthony Bradlee of political lore was now reduced to offering to run Mission District campaigns. Bradlee ordered a drink— a double Scotch—lit a cigarette and presented his fees. Victor was surprised; he expected them to be higher. More out of pity than commitment, Victor raised no objections to at least talking about being considered a candidate to challenge Meester. He could always back out after this meeting which seemed so important to Caballos, a man he admired, a man who had done a lot of good for the Mission District, a man with a preposterous Hispanic political dream.

In the background could be heard the metallic clank of a coin dropping through the jukebox. Bradlee spoke of demographics, of the ethnic vote, of schedules, of fund-raising, of organization. Bradlee, *the* Bradlee, the political pro, gave a careful analysis. A song began to play. In the middle of Bradlee's talk, Caballos turned to Victor and said, "I like this song. Don't you?" Victor, who was only half listening to Bradlee, turned to Caballos, nodded and smiled. "Yes, it's very pretty. It's *'Sin Ti,'* by El Trío Los Panchos."

"I know."

The two men smiled as Bradlee sipped his drink, kept talking, kept smoking. Strategies, smoke, words, Scotch and more words became intertwined. Bradlee was totally unaware of the beauty of the music, the words of the song and the glow of that singular musical moment being shared by Victor Lopez and Manny Caballos.

"Quite frankly I don't think Sergio stands a chance," said Bradlee, as a woman walked by their table leaving an odorous wake of cheap toilet water. "He's too . . . too . . ."

"Too much of a clown," said Caballos. "Speak of the Devil."

As if on cue, Sergio Barajas entered the restaurant like someone looking for a telephone to report a fire. Needless to say he was late. When he saw them there was great commotion, hands went up in the air, yells, profuse apologies. Some imbecile had blocked Barajas's car. "A beeg peek-op trok, *mano. ¿Qué tal?*" Bear hugs, slaps on the back, lavish handshakes. It was Sergio Barajas, Politician Barajas, Barajas the Clown, Barajas the Charlatan. He was wearing black pants and jacket and a cream-colored turtleneck sweater and a gold chain with a medallion which featured a gold pyramid with a dark eye in the center. His hair was tinted a reddish brown and his nails reflected manicure enamel. A flourish. A cock of the head. Arms out at his sides as if surrendering. Barajas had arrived. Barajas Triumphant, basking in political glory. He had just attended a political rally.

"They love-ed me," exclaimed Barajas with his thick accent. "There were Chinese and Filipinos and gays. We are all minorities," proclaimed Barajas. "Sixtee-fie percen of this city is minority or gay. Add the women, who love me, and you see how strong I am. I am going to win. Everywhere I go people tell me they will bote for me."

"What will you do if you get elected," asked Caballos.

"What do I do? *¿Quién sabe?* I haven't planned it out," said Barajas, bursting into laughter, coughing, grabbing Caballos by the elbow. Seeing that Caballos was not amused, he added, "I offer hope. I offer change."

"Change to what?" asked Caballos.

"Who knows? I haven't planned it out," said Barajas, laughing again. "I don wan to plan. I don wan to destroy. My administration will be bery . . . bery . . . creative. Politics is like music, like jazz. Jew know? Jew play it and jew change it and jew improvise it. Jew know? How is your lobly daughter, Manny? You know . . ."

"Celine?"

"Jes."

"O.K."

"Ees she steel goin with Tito Bastón?"

Barajas was probing a sore spot. What was Caballos to tell this moron? How much of the pain could he expose to him, and, besides, what did Barajas really care? Celine's relationship with Bobby Bastón had ended. Bobby Bastón had distressed her by sending a note that was snobbish and patronizing. The note declared that he wanted them both to be free, to grow. He was not ready to make a commitment, the kind Celine sought. He did not feel "mature enough" to take on the responsibility of an exclusive relationship. He spoke of Celine's beauty, her youth, of her need to evolve and explore, something he, too, needed.

Caballos had accidentally run across the note while looking for a pencil in Celine's desk. He didn't think much of
Bobby's words. *"¡Cagada!"* bellowed Caballos. "Nothing but
bullshit." Beneath all of Bobby's fine words, Caballos could
read what he had always suspected. Bobby Bastón did not
want to marry the daughter of a corn husk and Mexican beer
distributor. He suspected it at Judge Abelardo Quintana's
wedding when Bobby began giving his last name an English
pronunciation, accenting the first syllable in Bastón instead of
the last. He might have warned Celine but it would have been
useless. She would have accused him of being cynical. Besides,
she was too strong-willed and had been too much in love to
have listened.

Sometimes, in the middle of adding columns of figures,
she would stare away and he could tell what she was thinking.
Visions of sharing her life with Bobby, of singing to him, of
having his babies; visions of holding them in her arms would
appear and then dissolve before her. He remembered what it
was like when he had been rejected by a girl he had loved
desperately as a young man. It had been like losing a member
of the family. And there was nothing he could do. Caballos
wanted to hurt Bobby as much as he was now hurting his
Celine, his precious jewel. He wanted to threaten him, injure
him physically. But he quickly dismissed the thought. That
kind of thinking was for punks like Shark Salazar, not for a
businessman like himself. How could he try to force it? It was
as impossible to force people together as it is, in most cases, to
attempt to separate them. He had asked Celine if she wanted
to take a vacation, hoping that a change of scenery could help.
Without hesitating, Celine rejected the offer. And Celine had

wept. He never heard her. He never saw her. He didn't have to. It was there every morning in her eyes, in the redness of her cheeks, in the weight she was losing.

"Are she and Tito steel together?" Barajas insisted.

"No, they broke up."

"Oh, thet is too bed."

"She's not taking it well," said Manny Caballos.

"Oh, thet's good," said Barajas, looking away, not bothering to listen. Barajas's thoughtless response angered Caballos, but he quickly dismissed it as yet another piece of buffoonery from a quintessential buffoon.

A woman appeared. "Par' me." Barajas got up, went to her. He tilted his head and smiled, the surrendering hands went up in the air. A lavish hug, a fulsome kiss on the cheek. A tilt left. A tilt right. The woman was paying homage to Barajas, the next Mayor of the City and County of San Francisco. Barajas was ecstatic. He kissed her cheek and her forehead and then hugged her before she pulled away from him and left.

Barajas yelled out, *"Señor Blas!"*

Barajas saw that the Consul General from Mexico, Gil Blas, was leaving the restaurant. The Consul was fat, very light-complected and had light brown hair, thick lips and narrow eyes. He wore an expensive, tailored suit, from which protruded a pair of thick hands with fat fingers. Accompanying him were two very attractive, thin, young Latin women, wearing expensive clothes, which included spiked heels, and too much eye makeup and perfume. They looked around quickly, two sleek, tawny animals unaccustomed to confinement.

Barajas fluttered, went over to Blas. "Ah, Señor Blas.

How are jew? *¿Qué tal?*" Blas produced a careful smile and offered his hand limply, reluctantly. Regardless of his arrogance and his obvious dislike of Barajas, the Mexican Consul General in San Francisco could hardly refuse to shake the hand of a bona fide candidate for the office of Mayor of the City and County of San Francisco, no matter how silly the candidate. After all, Barajas had paid his election filing fees. Still he did not want his fine, expensive, pedigreed animals threatened or soiled by Barajas and he moved in front of them, shielding them. But Barajas would not be blocked. "I see jew are with two magneeficent, beauteeful women. Girls, are jew moobie stars or models?"

The women smiled weakly at Barajas and then looked at each other and then at the Mexican Consul General. Blas acknowledged Barajas the political candidate, Barajas the Clown, Barajas the Cur, and then brusquely moved on, "Good to see you, Sergio. I have a diplomatic matter to attend to," and he moved quickly past Barajas and through the crowded restaurant. He stopped briefly to talk to Bradlee and Caballos, and then moved on. The thin, dark women who were very graceful and very attractive—cheetahs in jeweled collars—walked very slowly, very carefully, in front of the Consul General, who was acknowledging other handshakes and other salutations. He dared not let them stray. It was as if the women at any moment would dart quickly for the door and be free.

An excited Barajas returned to the table looking at his watch, an elaborate chrome piece with three dials and a row of buttons. *"Aii, mira.* I forgot all about it. I meant to tell jew. I have an appointment at the *Chronicle.* I got to go. We'll have to talk some other time. O.K.?"

Caballos smiled. "Of course, Sergio. Chure," he added, imitating Sergio's thick accent.

"*Mira nomas.* Look at the time. I am already late. It is with all of the beeg chots at the *Chronicle.* They want to write about me. Good theen I lef Pepe in thee car. I hev to go. Geeb me a call, Tony." Handshakes all around. Apologies. "Good to see jew, Manny, and jew too, *carnal,*" he said, shaking Victor's hand, not remembering his name.

Barajas left the restaurant in another great flourish, waving, almost swooning, shaking hands, kissing another forehead, and then out and away in a flourish to the next scene in his own comic opera.

"A greater *pendejo* will be hard to find," said Caballos.

Bradlee was apologetic. "I thought he might be able to help," he said, draining his double Scotch and looking around for the waiter. "He's a Hispanic candidate. He has money. He knows the City."

Caballos flinched. And it became clear to Victor why the great Anthony Bradlee was now reduced to running a Mission District campaign.

The rest of the lunch was uneventful. Encouraged by Bradlee, Caballos spoke once again about his Hispanic Dream, of a Mexican John F. Kennedy in the White House, and Victor did not agree so much as raise no objections to his running as a candidate for the San Francisco Board of Supervisors. He would face Meester, a formidable, aggressive individual who was backed by the unions and who had a reputation for dirty campaigning. Victor sat back. The situation was impossible, very Mexican. In its own way it was even more hopeless than Sergio Barajas's campaign, which was little more than an obvious publicity stunt. Even Sergio acknowledged that. Victor sighed, half listening to Caballos; it was all such a dream. His campaign would be lackluster and forced. It would be run by a political hack who drank too much and who could not afford a new suit. It would undoubtedly be underfinanced and in the end, it would fail. He knew it and so probably did Bradlee. All to satisfy a lifelong dream harbored by the proud Manny Caballos; all to appease an aging man's dream. *Sea por Dios.*

In two days they would meet with Don Mario Castro to talk about campaign financing.

# Alexis Birdwell

**A**ii *mamacita*, thought Ruy, she's going to kill me.

# 16. Nights with Alexis

Alexis wears a thin, billowing dress. When she walks she appears enveloped in a black cloud. When he reaches for her she smiles and pulls away from him and begins to run. And he finds himself chasing her, out into an alley, a street, through a neighborhood and past an arching cat. The houses appear to be moving by him, tilting and bouncing as they pass. Cars, windows, people—all march past him eerily until he finds himself entering a dark rectangle, a neighborhood park, and the grass feels prickly against his bare feet. He can make out her figure in the moonlight pulling farther and farther away from him.

Stumbling, he chases her into a school playground past swings and monkey bars, and before he knows it he is stepping through sawdust and following her up into a net ladder that leads into the branches of a massive oak tree. The limbs of the tree appear like thick arms embracing the stars and the moon. It's a rope ladder that leads up to a children's tree house and the bright moon. He climbs the ladder anxiously, swaying with every step. Suddenly he drops down approximately five feet and finds himself entangled in the rope ladder, unable to move. He pulls his neck out of a tangle of rope.

How easily could he have killed himself, he thinks. His body would have been found by schoolchildren in the morning.

And Ruy begins to laugh as he looks up into the bright moonlit night, through the rope ladder, up through the branches of the oak tree, up beyond the stars into the blackness of the sky. He studies the pattern of the limbs on the tree. The moon appears to be caught in a web of limbs and branches and leaves.

Up there, somewhere above him, is Alexis in her billowing dress beckoning, and he tries to follow but he can't. His legs are tangled in the rope ladder and all he can do, all that is left, is laughter. She descends the rope ladder and approaches him. Her vanilla aroma precedes her. And after all of these months, all of the frustration, all of the heartache to find this woman who had been taunting him; after all of that, all he could do now is laugh. Alexis looks like a black widow spider about to devour her honeymoon-night suitor. She approaches him an inch at a time until her hair touches his face, and he feels like a happy insect caught in a web. She is over him and then next to him, devouring his mouth, removing his clothes. *Aiii, mamacita,* she's going to kill me, thinks Ruy, right here on the rope ladder beneath the stars and the moon. I am going to die, just like Mr. Birdwell did in Brazil. She hugs him and he begins to giggle, for he is ticklish. And then Alexis begins to giggle. And from some faraway place, something snaps and they find themselves dropping rump-first into a pile of very coarse sawdust. And then they both begin to laugh. From some other consciousness two flashlights approach, their beams scanning wildly. "Run!" she whispers, and Ruy, flushed, excited, half-dressed, finds himself running once again through a grassy field. Ahead of him, somewhere, beyond the lights of the city, in some other dream, is a silent, billowing form, Alexis, and he has to touch her. Ruy runs very hard, as hard as he can possibly run, and yet he can't reach her. She is fast and graceful. Soon he begins to throb and ache and perspire and he has to stop. Wheezing, he throws himself down on the grass and rests his back against the trunk of a tree, and he can hear the pounding of his own heart and breathing. And Alexis places her arms and legs around him and bites his lip. He returns her kiss and pushes away the folds of her billowing gown and he enters her and gazes into her eyes. She smiles and whispers, *"Mi hombre, hermoso."*

It's the happiest moment of Ruy's life.

# Marisol & Bunny García

Principals in the Marisol Emporium of Psychic Counseling and Healing.

# 17. Delfina Visits Marisol

Delfina waited impatiently for the Devil's reply to her offer. When two weeks passed without a word she became concerned and decided to take matters into her own hands.

She would visit the Marisol Emporium of Psychic Counseling and Healing, which was located in the International Pan American Building between Mission and Bartlett streets, the same building that housed the Alfonso Verdugo School of Spanish Dancing, the Graciela Escalante Beauty Salon and the Lilly Kong Fine Lingerie Boutique.

Marisol would know what to do. She was a gypsy from Morocco. She was also a psychic counselor and healer. Delfina was not sure what that meant so she looked up the word "psychic" in her dictionary to find the definition: "someone sensitive to nonphysical forces; one serving as a spiritualistic medium." Delfina still did not understand but since that didn't sound very Catholic, she decided that it meant someone who spoke to the Devil. She did not want to waste her time with some cheater who was only out to take her to the cleaners for her bundle.

As Delfina sat on a cane chair in the Marisol Emporium's small, dimly lit waiting room, she could smell sandalwood incense and make out the Persian rugs that covered the walls. A man emerged from behind a curtain. He looked sheepish and smiled awkwardly as he adjusted his belt and departed. And then she could hear a man and a woman arguing about insurance.

"Look, there are people who have to get paid to let you run this business."

"But you want twice as much as before."

"No, it's the guys downtown who want more. It's an election year. They're getting anxious. You know how they get around election time."

"*They* want more? Or do *you* want more?"

Suddenly Delfina recognized the male voice. It was the voice of that *ratero,* her own nephew, the *sinvergüenza,* the no-good Conde Pacheco.

"But this is robbery. I'm not paying."

"You have to pay or else."

"Or else what?"

"Or they may have to close you down."

" 'They'? 'Have to'? You bastard! Get out!"

"Be reasonable."

"Get out!"

"But, look . . ."

"Beat it!"

Conde Pacheco stalked out. He didn't notice Delfina and walked right past his own Tía Delfina without so much as a "Hello." Delfina frowned. She didn't know Conde Pacheco was in the insurance business. Probably another scheme to take people to the cleaners where he could get their bundle.

Delfina continued to wait. There was a small bar in the

waiting room and the magazines were different than the ones at the dentist's office: *Playboy, Penthouse* and *Sports Illustrated*— the swimsuit issue.

Delfina decided she had made a good choice. Nothing here looked the slightest bit Catholic. Marisol was the only person she could think of who could communicate directly with the Devil. Church was not such a good place. Everything there was blessed and besides Devils hated holy water; it extinguished them. Church was, however, the place where she had received her greatest inspiration: to question her religious beliefs and to make direct contact with the Prince of Darkness.

Bunny García, who happened to be on duty, peered at Delfina Varela through a peephole. She was not wearing the appropriate costume for a séance and changed out of a teddy to a woolen robe that smelled of pesto sauce—an item Marisol had picked up at a garage sale. Bunny added a thick veil and then escorted Delfina to a small, ill-lit room. At first Delfina could hardly see; after a minute she could make out bizarre symbols on the walls which she interpreted as representations of the Devil but which in reality were the signs of the zodiac. Yes, thought Delfina, she had made the right choice. Marisol knew Devil talk. Delfina could already feel the indecent excitement, the Devil's presence.

Bunny informed Delfina that the ordinary donation for a session was ten dollars. "We do not charge a fee for our services. Instead we ask you to make a donation of ten dollars."

"Just like at church," said Delfina. "They never ask you for money; they just ask you to make a little donation. If I do not make a little donation can Marisol still tell my fortune?"

"No."

Delfina, noting that the voice sounded familiar, opened her purse slowly, reluctantly, afraid to release something that would fly off or dart away forever. She extracted her wallet and cracked a Velcro strap revealing a faded photograph of a bald man with a moustache and a gold front tooth. Methodically, she put down a five-dollar bill, four one-dollar bills and then carefully counted out two quarters, two dimes, three nickels and thirteen pennies: $9.98.

"It's ten dollars," said Bunny García.

Delfina rooted about in the bottom of her purse and pulled out a small flashlight. "Ah, *mira,* there is that thing. I have been looking everywhere for it." She searched her purse and came up with a lint-covered stick of gum which she wiped on her sleeve.

"That will be fine," said Bunny García, accepting the donation, scooping bills, coins and gum into her hand and then disappearing.

Delfina strapped down her wallet and rearranged the contents of her purse, wondering what other long-lost item might be found there.

Marisol appeared in the dark room suddenly.

"*Aii,* Marisol, you scared me."

"Do not be afraid," said Marisol melodramatically. She wore a flimsy toga. Even in the dim light Delfina could make out Marisol's nipples through the material. "How can I be of service to you, Delfina? Is there something troubling you?"

"Well, I was just wondering, *sabes . . .*"

"Do you want to communicate with Panchito, your dearly departed husband?"

"No, no, let him rest in peace. I do not want to bother him. I do not want to get him involved."

"Do you wish to have your present life analyzed? Do you want me to cast a spell on someone."

"*Ya que* . . . What do I care about the present? And there's no one I want to hypnotize. Except maybe those two *metichis*, Dolores and Lucrecia. But I do not want to waste my ten bucks on those two."

Bunny García could be heard sniffling.

"Then you are interested in the future?"

"Well, yes, sort of . . ."

"Then let me see your right hand, please. Here, let me take your purse." Marisol reached to take Delfina's purse but Delfina gripped it tightly with both hands.

"That is all right. I would like to hold my purse. Thank you."

"Very well." Marisol took Delfina's callused right hand. "I see a life here of much labor. You have had to work very hard. The future will be less strenuous . . ."

"I do not know what that means."

"It means you won't have to work as hard."

"Do you see anything there about a car?"

"Huh?"

"What kind of car do you drive?"

"An Oldsmobile."

"How old is it?"

"It's this year's model."

"*Hijo.* You get a new car every year?"

"Yes."

"Business must be pretty good."

"Very."

"I didn't think there was so much money in fortune-telling."

"It's O.K."

"So let me tell you what's going on."

"Tell me."

"Well, you see, I want a *Cadiyác*. I prefer a new one, but I may have to settle for a used one. You see, I have this plan . . ."

Delfina related her plan to an astounded Marisol, who could hardly keep a straight face. She included all of the details. The front door chimes sounded and Bunny García could be heard greeting someone, a man who kept laughing nervously. Bunny's greeting was lavish, exaggerated. Marisol looked at her watch.

Delfina thought it sounded like Bunny García greeting the man; what in the world was she doing here? "When will I get my car?" asked Delfina.

Impatiently, Marisol responded. "You will get your car, Delfina."

"I will?"

"Yes. It will happen. I can see it here in this little line on your hand that goes to your heart. I can't make out if it's a Cadillac. But it *will* happen. I have never felt such a strong spiritual force."

"*¡Aiii, Chihuahua!*"

"I must go now, Delfina. I have another spiritual session. Come back and see me if you need more psychic counseling and healing. Thanks. You should go now."

"But why?"

"Another spiritual force may interfere with yours."

"Ah, *vaya.*"

"The door is that way. *Adiós.*"

"*Adiós.*"

"And next time the fee will be two hundred dollars. Our rates are going up. Bring the exact change next time. O.K.? Bye-bye."

"Bye-bye."

Delfina departed the Marisol Emporium of Psychic Counseling and Healing thinking that two hundred dollars an hour was a lot of money. No wonder Marisol could afford to get a new car every year. Delfina wondered if perhaps Marisol, herself, had made a pact with the Devil. Two hundred an hour? Delfina counted on her fingers. Two hundred times eight hours a day was . . . "*¡Aiii, chispas! That* was a lot of money."

That night she repeated those wonderful words over and over to her cat, Benjie, who was sound asleep. "You will get your car, Delfina. It will happen." She repeated the words hypnotically until she fell asleep, "You will get your car, Delfina . . . It will happen. You will get your car, Delfina. It will happen."

And then, in a dream, Delfina drove a shiny, pink Cadillac convertible past Señorita Lucrecia and Señorita Dolores, who pointed at her.

"*Madre Santísima.* Look! Who is that?"

"Why, it looks like Delfina Varela."

"What is she doing in a new car?"

"She must have stolen it."

"*Ave María Purísima.*"

Delfina smiled and rolled to one side. Her hand came to rest on Benjie's warm stomach.

# 18. Politics II:
# The Strategy Meeting

It was all so very un-Mexican: the meeting to discuss Victor Lopez's candidacy to the Board of Supervisors for the City and County of San Francisco. It was too logical; there was no emotion, no passion, no yelling. The meeting was held in the offices of Don Mario Castro, who smelled of perfume. Don Mario Castro was the President and Chief Executive Officer of the International Pan American Bank at Sixteenth and Mission streets. The restraint was unbearable. It was partly due to the futility of the cause—did anyone really believe Victor Lopez could beat Meester? But mostly the restraint was created by the setting.

Don Mario sat behind an imposing, marble-topped desk smiling like a benevolent dictator listening to a gathering of peasants who had come to claim his fertile land. On the table next to his right hand was a formidable letter opener, a dagger he had purchased in Seville used to administer the *coup de grâce* to dying bulls in a bullfight ring. And by his left hand was a row of buttons which, when pressed, would summon someone into his office immediately.

An entire wall was lined with photographs of Don Mario shaking hands with Presidents and royalty, Governors and industrialists, Hollywood personalities and cardinals. There were no toys in that office: no computers or fancy telephones or other electronic gadgets; a single telephone without buttons was on a table behind him.

Bradlee, the political strategist, spoke of potential problems, of financing, of Meester's strength, of his support by the unions, of his incumbency.

Ruy Lopez stared at a painting of two ballerinas behind Don Mario. His mind, as usual, was elsewhere, on the fragrance of Alexis, on the touch of her hair against his eyes, on her neck. On Winifred Lampson Birdwell, who was still in Brazil trying to sort out the financial muddle left by her late husband who had died the way every man should die: by having too much sex.

How absurd, thought Ruy. His little brother running as a candidate for the Board of Supervisors. It didn't make sense. Meester was simply too strong.

"But why, Victor? Why?" he had asked.

"*¿Quién sabe?*" was Victor's reply. Even Victor was unconvinced. It was all so futile, so very Mexican. Despite that, Ruy had offered to help his brother with his campaign.

"Anything you need, *mano:* licking stamps, addressing envelopes, passing out leaflets. Just do me one favor."

"What's that?"

"When you become President of the United States appoint me Secretary of Female Affairs."

Victor laughed. "*Vale,*" he said, tapping Ruy's clenched hand with his fist.

"*Vale,*" said Ruy, returning the tap.

Besides Bradlee, there was Manny Caballos, the relentless, implacable political dreamer, Judge Abelardo Quintana with his Adolf Hitler moustache, Terry Santamaría, the head of MAJA, and Ombligo the Fat, Ombligo the bureaucrat who headed a union of civil service and government employees whose endorsement was crucial to Victor's campaign.

Also attending was the delicate, effete lawyer Tito Torres, head of the Latino Political Action Congress. His suits were European. His words were well chosen. Beautiful English. Tito Torres served his words on a silver salver: lovely, delicious bonbons that one could relish and savor. He was light-complected and blond. He would have looked more at home at a meeting of the Sons of Norway than here. Manny Caballos had always wondered why Tito Torres chose to remain a Mission District lawyer and activist when he could so easily move to Mill Valley or Burlingame and double his legal fees; probably triple them if he changed his name. Perhaps it was only a front to give his organization a bit of Hispanic authenticity. He was a sly one, that Tito Torres. He knew how to capitalize on ethnic politics. Tito had his own agenda and he admitted it. He wanted a judgeship or to be appointed to a powerful state board like the Public Utilities Commission. By default, he would probably get what he wanted. Who could possibly feel threatened by a blond, blue-eyed Hispanic? Too bad he was married, thought Caballos. He would make an excellent husband for Celine, who was still in a state of melancholy over her breakup with Bobby Bastón.

Don Mario's sixteen-year-old daughter, Alicia Castro, walked in abruptly, not bothering to apologize. No one had invited her, she just simply appeared. Alicia was so muscular that she looked like a man. Her manner was brusque, graceless. Caballos looked at Alicia, at her pronounced moustache. How unlike Celine, he thought. What a big woman, and yet she would continue to grow; Alicia was scarcely sixteen.

"Dad, Mom wants some money," Alicia demanded, deflating Don Mario's austere dignity.

Don Mario tightened his lips as he fished in his pants pocket for his wallet, from which he pulled out a hundred-dollar bill, which he thrust at Alicia.

"Thanks." Alicia squashed the bill in her right hand and plodded out of the office, the laces dragging on her high-topped athletic shoes.

It was patently obvious that Alicia was an embarrassment to her father. Caballos offered a silent prayer thanking God for his own delicate Celine.

Bradlee continued and, as he spoke, attractive women—bank employees—walked up and down the hall past Don Mario's open door. As they passed, their high heels clicked on the red tiled floor. Occasionally, the smell of fine perfume wafted into Don Mario's office. To the men in the room the parade of aromatic women was a reminder of their implacable, relentless sensuality. The clicking heels—like the sounds of a clock—recalled once again their own daily, fallible carnality, and their easy vulnerability. Ruy Lopez looked out toward the hallway through the open door, at the sight of a woman passing by very quickly—a flash of stockinged thigh could be seen through a slit skirt. The site was breathtaking. Yes, he thought, sex would follow money and power as surely as pilot fish would follow sharks. But, Ruy wondered, why didn't Don Mario install a carpet to muffle the distracting sounds of the women's heels? Surely Don Mario could afford it. Ruy looked over at the white-haired Don Mario, who was sitting behind

his massive desk. Ruy smiled. The answer was obvious. Don
Mario cherished the sounds of those spiked and wooden heels
clicking like castanets on that tiled floor. He listened to those
musical notes all day and could probably identify the various
sounds made by the heels of his comely employees: María
Luisa and Carmen, Delia and Raquel, exotic houris in an old
man's dream. The good Catholic Ombligo kept his eyes away
from the doorway. It was Ombligo, finally, who could stand
the parade of sensuality no longer, that constant parade of
Hispanic girls with their long dark hair and heavy makeup,
dressed in tight pants or slit skirts.

"Do you mind if I close the door, Don Mario?"

Don Mario, slightly displeased, replied, "No, not at all."

A steering and finance committee was created for Victor
Lopez's campaign. Bradlee presented a timetable and a budget
as well as a fund-raising schedule. All went very quickly. No
one could question Bradlee's experience, Don Mario's influence or Manny Caballos's sincerity.

And that was the way Victor Lopez's hopeless campaign
for Supervisor for the City and County of San Francisco began.

Lunch was brought in dutifully by three pretty young
women. They dared not look up. The women were obviously
embarrassed to be serving the men. All Ruy could think of
was Egyptian slaves porting goods for their Pharaoh. Don
Mario looked at the women proudly, part of his stable of
handsome young animals put on earth to serve him. When the
women left, Don Mario pointed both palms at the food and
nodded, a gesture of benign obsequiousness, and the men ate
what was served: roast beef, tuna and egg salad sandwiches,
apples and oranges.

Another woman walked in with beverages. She wore a

pair of very tight white pants and a black, ruffled blouse. Ruy assessed her figure, the tight pants, the curving bottom. He inhaled, smiled; a bright thought appeared. At times, rarely, life could be so lovely, a sweet tune played on a guitar. And then, uncontrollably, it played itself out once again: the smell of vanilla, Alexis throwing her head back in laughter as her bare, oiled bottom, slightly propped, glistened defiantly in an afternoon sun.

And then another image of Alexis fanned across his memory like shuffled playing cards.

Alexis holding a yellow pear in her long fingers. There's red polish on her sharp fingernails. She raises the fruit to her burgundy lips and then bites down into the flesh of the fruit very slowly, all the while looking directly into Ruy's astonished eyes. Her eyes are dark, exotic, almost Oriental in that light. Ruy shudders. She looks like an animal, something wild devouring a helpless, trapped creature, which Ruy indeed was. Would she one day hold his staff in her hand that same way and consume it whole and entire while staring into his eyes?

"Why me?" he asks.

"Why not?" Alexis replies. An answer in the form of a question that perplexes Ruy. "Just accept it for what it is, Ruy," says Alexis. "Nothing more; nothing less. When it happens it just happens. When it's very good it can be beautiful. Just share it with me, please, and don't question it. O.K.?"

"O.K."

It's all too complex. Ruy can say no more. He won't destroy the relationship by trying to define it, by questioning it. But, in his heart of hearts, he knows that there's no answer.

And he knows the relationship will never last.

Once again the dance begins as Alexis embraces him and unbuttons his shirt. She kneels before Ruy and for an instant she appears like a supplicant serving her master. But this illusion fades as Ruy also kneels and Alexis gives him that powerful kiss he remembers so well from that very first night.

For Alexis it was sex, always the sex. She was implacable, insatiable. She wanted sex, nothing but sex, time and again. Sex in all of its manifestations: outdoors, indoors; under water and above; prolonged eternally or quick and often. North, South, East and West. Now sweet and gentle, now rude and vulgar. Sometimes it was wild, almost violent; sometimes soft and innocent. Now she was a kitten, coy and affectionate, now she was a cornered lynx slashing at Ruy's exposed back, her green eyes glaring, ready to repeat it all again and again, and then again and again. A little girl dressed in white reaches a tongue up to receive her First Holy Communion, as a street-wise harlot reaches a tongue past her red, waxy lips to remove a crystal drop from the tip of Ruy's throbbing erection. Now it was all silent and subdued, now it was brilliant and noisy. Now a minuet on a harpsichord, now a punk rocker's scream to an electric guitar chord. Gentleness, savagery. Velvet, barbed wire. Jagged obsidian and spongy moss.

Until, inevitably, it all began to fuse together into a tumbling round of dissipation and exhaustion. Ruy began to wonder if he too would die like Winifred Lampson Birdwell's late husband.

"Ruy, *amigo,* you are suffering from exhaustion. Your nerves are shot. What are you doing to yourself?" asked Dr. Mateo Figueroa.

Ruy had looked into Dr. Figueroa's drooping, sad eyes. He seemed perpetually grief-stricken. He was such a kind, gentle man. How could he possibly tell him, and if he did, how could he understand? How could he tell him about Alexis; about her insatiable lust, her slashing nails, her frenzied tongue, her beautiful body. Dear Dr. Figueroa. Dear God. What could he say? What should he do?

"No doubt you're thinking too much about her."

Ruy snapped awake. "Who?"

"Amapola. Her leaving you has probably affected you."

"Yes, of course."

"Maybe you should try to get a girl friend. You are a healthy man with certain basic appetites that should not be denied."

Ruy smiled. Dear Dr. Figueroa. "Yes, of course."

# The Used Chevy

Delfina Varela figured that at her age she'd probably have
to settle for a Chevrolet, perhaps even a used one.

# 19. Delfina Varela's Own Strategies

Delfina Varela's two-story Victorian house was so small that a one-car garage made up the entire first floor. She and her late husband, Panchito, had paid $8,000 for the unit when they first moved into the Mission District, an astronomical sum, at the time, that had taken them decades to pay off. They had fallen in love with the tiny house on Ortigalita, a street that was lined with bottlebrush trees and plum trees whose leaves were purplish black. A bougainvillea plant, whose thick trunk originated in a small flower bed, arched across the front of the structure and appeared to be embracing it in a thick mantle of reddish-purple flowers.

One bright, sun-filled Sunday morning, following a night of Cadillac dreams, Delfina Varela decided to prepare for the arrival of her new car. She opened the garage door to find years of accumulated junk: a cracked mirror, stacks of old magazines, pieces of faded furniture, broken garden tools. She raised the lid of an old trunk to encounter the smell of mothballs and layers of old clothing. Panchito's old love letters were in a bundle that was neatly tied with a red ribbon. Delfina touched one piece of clothing nostalgically: a faded black and red negligee Panchito had given her. Perhaps she would keep the negligee and Panchito's letters. All the rest she would get rid of to make room for the new car. "The new car!" The words sounded magical.

A few days later a junk dealer removed most of the remaining items. "My God, you've got a lot of shit here, lady."

"It is not chit. It is the *momentos* of my life."

"Mementos?"

"Mementos. *Ya que.* You call them chit because you do not want to pay me what they are worth. I am not a dummy."

The rest she had hauled and dumped. Delfina swept out the entire garage, raising clouds of dust, and then wiped the walls, shelves and ceiling with a damp cloth. She even washed and waxed the concrete garage floor. She would put a nice dark curtain against the small window to protect the car from the afternoon sun. On the long shelf that ran along one wall, she would place the car cleansers and polishes. Clean washcloths and a new chamois cloth would hang neatly on little hooks. She would wash the car on the street in front of the garage where everyone could see her new car. Maybe Señorita Dolores and Señorita Lucrecia would walk by just as she was wiping her new *Cadiyác* with a fine chamois cloth. Delfina relished the thought.

"Hello, Delfina. Why are you working on Sunday, the Day of the Lord?"

"I am washing my new *Cadiyác.*"

"*Your* new *Cadiyác?*"

"Yep."

"And where did you get the car?"

"The Devil gave it to me."

Boy, that would really be something. Delfina could see them now, standing there, their mouths open, ready to drop their false teeth. One or the other would have to say, *"Ave María Purísima."*

The thought of shocking Dolores and Lucrecia warmed Delfina. She inhaled deeply. She smiled appreciatively. She could almost smell the car, the cleansers, the wax, the gasoline and the oil, and the breathtaking, wonderful smell of exhaust fumes. The car interior would smell sweet and clean. She would buy a small basket for Benjie, which she would put on top of a box on the passenger seat so that he could look out when she drove. She would even purchase a car deodorizer board shaped like a flat little green pine tree which she would hang from the rearview mirror. It would be very stylish. That is where the punks in the "boom" cars always hung their little deodorizer trees.

Delfina decided she would always leave the garage door open to make it easier for the Devil to park her new car. Above the garage door Delfina hung a hand-lettered sign whose letters were rendered in red paint. The sign read,

NO PARKING EVER
THIS MEANS YOU MISTER
YOU WILL BE SORRY

She looked at the sign, cocking her head to the left and then to the right and then nodded and smiled as Benjie the cat appeared to rub himself against her ankles. "There you are, you naughty boy, where have you been? I have been looking all over for you. I have something to tell you." Delfina informed Benjie that he would have to stay with their neighbor, Señora Talavera, for a few days. "You know how you like her chicken in *mole* sauce, Benjie. It is good for you," Delfina told Benjie, who became very upset that she would have to leave town. "I have to go to Fresno to see Chencha. This time she got sick from the chingles. I have to take the bus. *¡Qué pena!* With my *juanetes* it will not be easy. See, Benjie, when we get the new car we will both go together to see Chencha." Benjie offered Delfina a forlorn meow. *"Aiii,* don't worry, *gatito,* Señora Talavera will take good care of you, *precioso.* I will be back as soon as I can.

"*¡Hijo 'e la!*" said Delfina, as she picked up the cat. "You must weigh a ton." The truth was that the spoiled cat now weighed nineteen pounds.

# The Basilica of Mission Dolores

From which saints, angels and other deities looked down sternly . . .

# 20. O Mary, We Crown Thee

"O Mary, we crown thee with blossoms today,
"Queen of the Angels, Queen of the Day."

It was another spellbinding Catholic ceremony in the Basilica of Mission Dolores. It was all there once again, unchanging, enduring: the guilt-inspiring Crucifixion scene, the stained-glass windows, the wooden pews that smelled of furniture polish, the oversized statues with big feet, the marble baptismal font. The altar linens were immaculate: white and starched. As usual, there were too many flowers, too many candles. It was ceremony. It was Catholic. It was the annual Queen of the Flowers ceremony which would culminate in the crowning of the statue of the Blessed Virgin Mary by this year's Flower Queen, Don Mario's daughter, Alicia Castro.

Father *In*Clemente was glowing with pride and booze. His idea had been nothing less than brilliant, an amazing flash of inspiration. To please one of the biggest contributors to church causes he had chosen Alicia as this year's Flower Queen. Alicia Castro, the daughter of Don Mario the banker,

Don Mario "The Prince of the Mission District." Father *In-Clemente* smiled. It was a true stroke of genius. He could hardly contain himself. He was also very proud of his new organist, Clinton.

The crowning of the statue by Alicia would follow a First Holy Communion ritual in which boys in black suits and girls in white dresses and veils would, for the first time in their lives, participate in the Sacrament of the Holy Eucharist. They would receive their First Holy Communion in the form of a slender, tasteless wafer containing the body of Jesus Christ.

The non-Hispanic Clinton was playing the organ recklessly, a phantom in his own opera.

*"Qué raro,"* said Señorita Dolores as Clinton shook the foundations of the church more effectively than Martin Luther or a 7.1 earthquake. Clinton felt that Hispanics could only reach God through loudness. Perhaps he had a point.

"Cleen-ton is playing like a man possessed," said Señorita Lucrecia.

"Something's got him," replied Señorita Dolores.

*"Órale, ya que.* Maybe the guy should calm down."

Everyone knew there was something peculiar about the tall, skinny Clinton, whose disheveled blond hair looked as if it had been combed by an exploding firecracker. For one thing, went the logic, no sane non-Hispanic would so totally participate in such grossly Hispanic functions. And besides, ordinary people did not play the organ that way. Clinton tended to curl over the keyboard like a hunchback and kick his feet at the pedals in all directions.

"Look at him," said Señorita Lucrecia. "He looks like a chicken being strangled."

*"Qué raro."*

"No one should be that pale, that white."

"He must live in a cave and grow mushrooms."

"Wild mushrooms."

In a community where bright colors and swarthy complexions were esteemed, Clinton's anemic complexion was looked upon with great suspicion, further proof of his madness.

Between Clinton on the organ and the perpetually besotted Father *In*Clemente at the altar, the ceremony that day would take on a surrealistic air.

Dressed in a wedding gown, Alicia was to climb a ladder and place a wreath of baby pink roses on the head of the statue of the Blessed Virgin Mary. The dainty statue sat on a high platform surrounded by so many flowers that its entire lower half was completely hidden. Mary looked like a hunted jungle creature surrounded by dense foliage as she peeked through rings of flowers at her stalker: Alicia Castro.

Alicia was chosen to be Queen of the Flowers not for her academic excellence. Of the grades on her monthly report cards her father would often yell, "A donkey could do better than this!" And she was certainly not chosen for her beauty; Alicia had a pronounced moustache and was so muscular—her favorite pastime was lifting weights—that she looked like a man in drag. Her large feet, more accustomed to high-topped tennis shoes with dragging shoelaces, were ready to pulverize her enormous white satin high-heeled shoes.

The real reason Alicia had been chosen Queen of the Flowers; the real reason she was now in agony dressed in a wedding gown ready to crown the statue of the Blessed Virgin Mary, was her father's generous contributions to a number of church causes. Father *In*Clemente may not have been temperate but he was no dummy. Through his torpid stupor, the priest smiled at Alicia and then at her father, Don Mario, sitting proudly in one of the forward church pews.

Came the moment.

Clinton the Unfettered, Clinton the Liberated. The organ was vibrating the congregation's diaphragms and loose dentures. The procession of the innocents was about to begin. All of the children who had received the Sacrament of the Holy Eucharist, their First Holy Communion, lined up at the back of the church and began walking up the center aisle. They were followed by several altar boys dressed in white cassocks and torchbearers wearing red. These in turn were followed by several members of the Knights of Columbus, including Don Mario, who carried a heraldic banner. At the end of the parade were two rows of very young, very dainty girls, who carried small bouquets of flowers, wearing white frilly dresses and Mary Jane shoes; and then came the flagship, the hippopotamic Alicia looking tortured and in pain, proceeding unsteadily as she ground her thick feet into her high-heeled satin shoes.

The procession had majesty, dignity. Clinton finally composed himself long enough to allow the angelic voices of the children to be heard.

"O Mary, we crown thee . . ."

The church bells rang. Don Mario was in a trance. Perhaps there could be hope for his husky weight-lifting daughter with her big feet and the face and body of a man. There was time. She was young. Young people got over fads. Maybe he could send her to a fat farm in Hilton Head, get her moustache, armpits and pubic area plucked. Maybe a little plastic surgery here and there. Hell, why not? He could afford it. Alicia was a good girl. Perhaps she could meet some nice young man . . .

His thoughts were interrupted.

One of the dainty young girls in the procession began to vomit into her lace gloves. Her mother quickly ran to her and removed the puking child from the stifling church. Father *In*Clemente saw the small episode and continued to smile benignly. The entire thing seemed so natural, so primitive to him; so much a part of these lavish ceremonies. The whole thing was so . . . so Mexican. He was proud to be here.

The procession made it to the front of the church and then circled around the statue of the Blessed Virgin Mary, as two of the altar boys began to giggle uncontrollably after one whispered to the other, "She looks like Arnold Schwarzenegger in drag."

The children sang:

"O Mary, we crown thee with blossoms today,
"Queen of the Angels, Queen of the Day."

Amalia Alegre's new baby—the pink baby girl born on the floor of the Mission Dolores Parish Hall—began to cry. She was getting bored with the song. She screamed as if a white-hot poker had been inserted into her great intestine. Don Mario blew his nose triumphantly into a blue silk handkerchief. Señorita Lucrecia and Señorita Dolores wiped away tears as Alicia, carrying the crown of baby pink roses, ascended the ladder behind the statue with great difficulty. Clinton closed with another cannonade on the organ, and then only the voices of the children could be heard almost as whispers.


"O Mary, we crown thee with blossoms today,
"Queen of the Angels, Queen of the Day."


Amalia's baby cried out.

At the very top of the ladder, Alicia Castro raised the crown of flowers as high as she could above the statue. And then she screamed as her massive foot erupted through her right shoe, causing her to lose her balance. People gasped. For a second it looked as though Alicia would regain her balance as she swung back and then forward grabbing at the statue. To no avail. Both Alicia and the statue tumbled forward into a mass of flowers and wreaths and her father's disgust. *Mierda,* thought Don Mario. Why did I ever let that boozer talk me into this embarrassment? Father *In*Clemente kept smiling. He wanted to present a show of composure amidst chaos. Instead what he presented was a show of inebriated listlessness.

*"Borrachento,"* barked Señorita Lucrecia.

"Drunkard," echoed Señorita Dolores.

Screams filled the church. Children began to cry. Men rushed to the fallen Alicia, who on the way down had demolished the entire platform that was holding the statue and vases of flowers. Pulling away flowers and branches, they found both Alicia and the statue intact.

As Father *In*Clemente reached for her, Alicia pushed him away and yelled in perfectly articulated English, "Get your hands off of me, you drunken son-of-a-bitch!"

"What did she say?" asked Señorita Dolores.

"I think it was something naughty," said Señorita Lucre-cia.

"I know, but what did she say?"

"I believe she just called Father *In*Clemente a drunken son-of-a-bitch."

*"Aiii, Dios mío."*

As men pushed away flowers, ferns and rank water from both Alicia and the toppled statue, the two altar boys began to laugh uncontrollably.

Amalia Alegre's baby gurgled sweetly and then smiled radiantly at her mother before yawning and falling asleep.

# 21. A Disaster Befalls Señor Caballos

Manny Caballos slammed both palms into his forehead. He could not believe the sight before him. His lovely, perfect jewel, his Celine, was riding a motorcycle with the Punk, Shark Salazar. Oh, God, please, he mourned. She could have her pick of any man she wanted and yet, there she was riding on the back of a motorcycle with Shark Salazar. Why, he was nothing but a two-bit drummer. When he wasn't pounding the drums, he worked in an automobile shop painting orange and maroon flames on motorcycle gas tanks or pinstriping cars that lowriders liked to drive. How could she do this to him? He couldn't believe the sight before him. Celine was sitting behind Shark, hugging his waist. Her dress had climbed up to her own waist, revealing her fine, slim, white legs and thighs and even bits of her underwear. As they drove by, Celine looked directly at her father.

Later, Caballos confronted Celine. He scolded and ranted and accused Shark of being no good, the head of a gang of dangerous punks.

"It's only a band," said Celine, "nothing more. They're very good musicians and they make very good money."

"I don't give a damn," hollered Caballos. He warned Celine that her own reputation was at stake along with that of the entire Caballos enterprise. He reminded her that she was now a business partner. He was stunned to learn how long they had been seeing each other. He spoke of Shark as a criminal and a hoodlum.

In a softer tone, Caballos acknowledged that Celine had been hurt by Bobby Bastón—"that faggot"—but that Shark was not the answer. He pointed out Celine's long sadness, her vulnerability, the fact that Shark—the very name seemed to be stabbing him—was probably the first person to offer her a sympathetic ear, besides himself, of course. The ranting lasted most of an hour, during which time Celine said little. "I want you to stop seeing Shark Salazar," Caballos finally insisted, doing all he could to control his voice, his temper.

Celine gathered her purse and sweater, went to the door and said coldly, "You present a valid argument. I'll think about it," and walked out; she was late for a date with Shark Salazar. Caballos was incensed, as much by the thought of his daughter seeing the punk, *that* Punk, as by the coldness of her answer. He knew what that meant. Caballos felt trapped. What would happen to Caballos and Son and Daughter? Would it all fold because of Shark Salazar? Caballos uttered a silent, sincere prayer. Tomorrow he would go to mass and pray to God for an end to this outrage.

But praying didn't help.

Two days later, Celine asked to have a meeting with her father, a request he ducked. He was able to delay the confrontation by taking an unnecessary week-long business trip to Los Angeles.

When he returned, she was waiting.

"Father, I have something to tell you," Celine announced.

Caballos could not bear to hear it. He closed his eyes. He could hear himself inhale. He faced his daughter and stared into her eyes. There was steel there, a determination he knew only too well. He looked past her, out to his own youth, to the streets of East Los Angeles, to the Chinese restaurants and their unforgettable smells, to faded, brown photographs of his beautiful young mother who now lived in a sanitarium and who no longer recognized him. He thought most of all of his late wife, his dear Esperanza. He knew what Celine would say. He could not bear to hear it. He looked out to a sea of dreams, of dark children, of golden, rolling hills flecked with green oak trees. He wanted to hear the sounds of the sea. Anything, anything but this. All of this played itself out in his mind for an eternity, for a few brief seconds, as Celine cleared her throat. The blow struck him directly.

"I'm going to marry Shark Salazar." He suddenly felt very tired and old, completely useless. She wasn't even asking him; she was telling him. Caballos closed his eyes and said nothing. There was nothing he could do to stop her; there was nothing he could say. *Sea por Dios.*

That afternoon, Manny Caballos entered the back yard of his Dolores Street home to be pleased yet again by the look and sound of his elegant, small garden with its beds of roses and a small, trimmed lawn and rows of hedges which were kept green and clipped. Off in a corner of the garden, by a statue of St. Francis of Assisi, a fountain burbled musically. Behind the fountain was a small, bougainvillea-covered grotto and a faded photograph of his late wife taken when she was in her teens. The black-and-white photograph had been colorized. Esperanza's wavy hair glistened, her thin lips were red and her cheeks were rose-colored. In the weathered photograph she was turning sideways, looking up, always looking up, always turning sideways. Father *In*Clemente had blessed the grotto which, in Caballos's mind, had made Esperanza's stained photograph sacred, a sanctioned object of worship.

Caballos knelt slowly on a weathered pew. He felt very tired as he whispered a small prayer to his departed wife. The words were not easy. "Celine wants to marry Shark Salazar . . ." Shark's name caught in his throat like a fish bone. Caballos could not go on. He reentered his immaculate two-story Victorian home filled with color and light and the smell of coriander and oregano, nutmeg and cinnamon, herbs and spices which became mingled in his mind with the rich memories and earthy smells of Esperanza. The old sounds reappeared: closing doors, opening windows, footsteps, running water, curtains being drawn, whispers; and always, always, Esperanza's singing.

Sinking into a soft leather chair in the spacious living room, Caballos examined his home as if for the very first time. He remembered how he and Celine and Carlos had toiled to refurbish it. A mint-green rug, which covered most of the floors of the house, had been removed, revealing splendid oak floors which they had sanded, stained and varnished. A painted fireplace mantel was stripped to reveal a soft green and milk-white marble. A domed ceiling in the dining room had become Celine's special project. She had painted the ceiling with scenes of Spanish conquistadors and pre-Columbian deities emerging from pastel clouds; fat-rumped cherubs held golden trumpets from which trailed iridescent ribbons, and rhesus monkeys frolicked with dancing children wearing short gowns. The corners contained scenes of California mission buildings and Franciscan monks laboring with Indian workers in green fields of corn. The great god Quetzalcoatl, besieged by sublime comely maidens, had often looked down approvingly at dinners punctuated by conversation and laughter and, invariably, a song by Esperanza which often followed a glass or two of Caballos's homemade brandy. Children had routinely been mesmerized staring at the wondrous scenes on that dining room ceiling.

Caballos recalled how Carlos had found a house being demolished and had bought a number of stained, leaded and faceted windows. These had been placed in windows throughout the Caballos house with the most exquisite one going into the upper panel of a huge front door made of oak. The scene in this window depicted Renaissance hunters in pursuit of a stag surrounded by dogs. The scene had been etched on white, opaque glass with small accents of emerald green flecked throughout. The scene's borders consisted of small, diamond-shaped pieces of brilliant scarlet glass. This window set the tone for entry into the house. When Caballos first saw the hunting scene he was saddened at the sight of the cornered stag. "Poor thing, doesn't stand a chance," he said, and every time he entered that front door he uttered a small prayer for the survival of the cornered stag. Only later did Caballos discover that his big dumb son, Carlos, had used savings meant to buy a car to purchase those windows.

He and Carlos and Celine had worked diligently to restore the small house. Esperanza had helped, as had neighbors and friends. Total strangers volunteered to help complete the project, which acquired its own exuberant momentum and became a neighborhood cause. And when the magnitude of the project became clear to Caballos, he flew to Mexico to buy exquisite wrought-iron lamps from Tlaquepaque as well as fine brass doorknobs and bathroom fixtures in Guadalajara. When the house remodeling was completed and new coats of paint had been applied, he hired a Swiss landscape architect by the name of Hans Dietricht Leute to lay out a precise garden that included tulip and liquidambar trees, roses and shrubs, bougainvillea and jasmine as well as Caballos's coveted grotto and bubbling fountain.

Caballos was proud of his elegant house with its beautiful doors and windows and perfect hedges and bougainvillea-covered grotto. So overwhelmed was he when he saw the finished product that he sat down and cried. When Carlos attempted to comfort him, Caballos pushed him away and said what men always say when they cry, "I'll be all right."

And afterwards, with the paint dry and the hedges clipped, Caballos threw a magnificent party. He hired a *maria-chi* band whose trumpets, violins and guitars filled the neighborhood for blocks around with glory and triumph. Bunny García and the gypsy Marisol played guitars and sang love songs, and everyone had enjoyed Bunny's persimmon cookies and his own sweet, spiked cider. Even Father *In*Clemente had been invited. He was not allowed to drink the cider until after he had blessed the house, the statue of St. Francis of Assisi, the grotto and Esperanza's photograph. Only when this sacred chore was completed was he allowed to taste Caballos's fine cider; only then did he begin to smile foolishly and say unintelligible things, and everyone knew that Father *In*Clemente was inebriated once again, lost in his own special world of glazed incoherence and muffled pain. It had been a perfect day. No one in all of the Mission District had ever seen a more beautifully restored home.

Caballos tried praying to Esperanza once again and all he could think of was the terrible way her family had objected to their own marriage. Esperanza's father had threatened to disown her because of Caballos's poverty and breeding, his lack of education and his vulgarity—the same things Caballos now despised about Shark Salazar. Caballos felt crushed, overwhelmed, defeated. Her father had no doubt felt as he did right now. Perhaps it was the fate of all fathers to be sadly disappointed, he thought. It took years of marriage before her family would even talk to him. It had not been easy on Esperanza. Is this what he would impose on Celine, whose will could be obstinate and unbending? Caballos walked through the rooms of his house. He could hear Esperanza singing a whimsical song, *"El Bigote de Tomás,"* or "Tom's Moustache," and Caballos smiled. Esperanza, as always, was telling him to be kind.

# 22. A Proposal

There, on the back of the hand, in the area between the thumb and forefinger, was a smiling bunny rabbit holding a daisy in one paw. Manny Caballos often thought that perhaps the last thing he would see in this life would be that hand, with the bunny rabbit tattoo, thrusting a knife at him or hurling a hand grenade into his precious home. That hand appeared on Caballos's desk that morning. Caballos looked up. It was Shark Salazar and he was smiling. What a perfect smile, thought Caballos, what perfect teeth. Shark could be disarming with that smile. Little wonder Celine could fall for him. He had enthusiasm, he was handsome and he possessed a powerful weapon: that perfect, sparkling smile that radiated across his entire face and shone in his eyes and cheeks. That and the terrible facial scar that added danger and excitement to the effect. Who could resist that perfect smile? Who could deny this scarred puppy?

Jesus Christ! What the hell was he thinking about? This punk was out to seduce his daughter, his precious prize, his most beloved, magical angel. What was the matter with him? Shark was out to fuck his own daughter and in the process fuck over his entire business. What the hell was he thinking about?

"What the hell do you want?" asked Caballos.

Undeterred by the abrupt greeting, Shark's smile persisted. "I have a proposition for you, Señor Caballos . . ."

What an amazing smile, thought Caballos, the smile of a con man. Caballos crossed his arms, leaned back to hear Shark's proposal.

"I want to join the business," said Shark.

"What business?"

"Your business."

Caballos snapped forward. His immediate reaction was anger, violence; but then he recalled his own youthful audacity. It was exactly the way he had gotten started. He and Shark were cut from the same cloth: direct, indiscreet, impatient. Caballos felt his anger turn to amusement. It was as if he were confronting a young version of himself.

Shark's boldness was appealing. Suddenly Caballos found himself smiling. "You do, do you? Tell me, why?"

"Because I've listened to Celine talk about the business. It's healthy. It's good; but it could be even better. She tells me you'd like to retire."

"So. You two want to push me out?" Caballos was baiting Shark.

"Of course not, Señor Caballos." Unflustered, Shark continued. "You and Celine run a profitable business. But you could do even better with a bit of sales and marketing, something you've never done. I'd like to take on that role. I'd like to do your sales and marketing. I'd also like to work with Carlos, involve him in more of the business. Carlos and I get along well."

Caballos had to agree, for the truth was that Carlos adulated Shark, his music, his charisma. Involving Carlos in more of the business was one of Caballos's dreams. He had never found the time. Shark was touching one of Caballos's dearest hopes: to see his only son emerge as Celine's true business partner instead of merely stacking boxes and making deliveries. Shark continued, presenting a precise plan which was practical, possible; the same neat logic used by Celine. She had obviously coached him; he was using many of her very words, "feasible," "prudent," "expedient."

"And when you feel you're ready to retire we can talk about my buying into the business, Señor Caballos, if everything works out."

The amusement drained from Caballos's face. "Where the hell are you going to get the money to buy into my business?"

"I've saved the money from my band gigs. I manage to live mostly on the money from my job at the paint shop."

"Would you be ready to put up $25,000?" Caballos, who loved to play poker, produced the figure as a bluff. He wanted to see Shark's reaction.

Without hesitating, Shark responded. "No, I can't. Not all of it. Not now. But I *can* cover some of it, most of it *now.*" Celine had coached him well, thought Caballos. Shark hadn't blinked; he hadn't swallowed. "And I can raise the rest; it wouldn't be hard, Señor Caballos." Shark refused to drop the formality. He was one of the few people Caballos knew who didn't immediately start calling him "Manny" two minutes after meeting him.

"But why do you want into this kind of business?" Caballos asked. "You're doing your own thing. You've got your own band."

"Because I'm serious about Celine. Because I'm looking toward my own future and hers; our future together." Shark's voice was firm, passionate. These were his words now, not Celine's. "Because I want to buy into an established business, one that presents a good opportunity to increase my band's gigs. While marketing the products of Caballos and Son and Daughter I can make valuable contacts and probably increase the engagements for the band. Besides, to be honest, there's only a certain half-life to any band before it gets stale. We're not Los Lobos. We've never cut an album or even a single record. We have no illusions about ourselves. We're a decent Latin band that can carry a beat, play loud music and get people to dance. That's all we are. I'm thinking of our long-term future, my future and Celine's. Long-term, I don't think that a guy working in clubs filled with drunks and smoke would make a very good family man. One of my goals is to raise a family."

Caballos couldn't respond; he needed time. He put on his glasses to look at Shark. For once, he looked beyond Shark's terrible scar, beyond the bunny rabbit tattoo, beyond his own prejudices. Shark made perfect sense. He presented his argument well and his logic was impeccable, even without Celine's coaching. No wonder they got along. And there again was Shark's infectious smile.

As if in a poker game, Caballos raised the stakes. He would call Shark's bluff. Caballos made a counterproposal. "Try it for three months on a voluntary basis. If you can show me increased profits and prove to me that you, me, Celine and Carlos can all work together well, I'll consider your offer. Seriously."

"And what about my engagement to Celine?"

Caballos tightened his lips. He had to push Shark away. "Don't push your luck."

"Whatever you say, Señor Caballos," said Shark as he turned to leave.

Caballos stopped him. "One more thing."

"What?"

"Call me 'Manny.' "

"Sure"—Shark felt embarrassed saying it—"Manny."

*"Vale, carnal,"* said Caballos, pulling the vocabulary out of his East Los Angeles past.

*"Vale,* Manny," said Shark, producing his radiant smile and offering to shake Caballos's hand. Instead, Caballos embraced him and the two men slapped each other's back in a Mexican hug.

When Shark left, Caballos allowed his mind to drift away once again into some of his most cherished thoughts. Perhaps he *could* retire; perhaps Carlos could get involved more in the business. Maybe, just maybe, he *could* begin to think seriously of devoting more time to his favorite political fantasy, the dream of seeing a Mexican-American President of the United States of America in the White House, a Mexican John F. Kennedy with a bristling moustache. The thought warmed him. Caballos removed his glasses to look out to a sea of dreams, of dark children, of golden, rolling hills flecked with green oak trees. He could almost hear the sounds of the sea. Victor Lopez's campaign was going well. Perhaps there *could* be hope.

# 23. The Telephone Call

While in Supervisor von Meisterding's office, Conde Pacheco answered a telephone call.

"Hey? Conde? How's it going? Can you talk?"

"Hold on." Conde put down the telephone to close the office door. "Damy! Jesus Christ, why are you calling me here at City Hall? Your call could be traced."

"Don't worry, Conde, I'm calling from a pay phone."

"I heard what happened to you, Damy. Every cop in the city's looking for you."

"Yeah, I know. I really fucked up this time."

"God, I'll say. Did you have to shoot him?"

"Well, he was going to search the car and then, you know, things kind of got out of hand."

"Yeah, but the fact is you shot a cop."

"Man, don't make it sound like I'm a serial killer. How is he?"

"He's in critical condition. I heard it on TV. Oh, my God, Damy, you'll get killed dealing dope."

"No lectures, man. I need help."

"What?"

"A place to . . ."

Conde interrupted. "Well, you sure as hell can't stay with me. Lourdes would freak out. Our marriage is already stressed to the breaking point. And how would it look? I shouldn't even be talking to you. You could really screw things up for me and for Supervisor von Meisterding. There's a special election going on. Or haven't you heard?"

"Conde, my man, you don't understand. I don't need a lecture, I just need a place to hide my wheels for a while. That's all. It's like a bull's-eye to every cop in town. I need your help."

"Why come to me? I can't help you."

"Like *hell* you can't. Man, I've done you *beaucoup* favors."

"I'll see what I can do. Let me get back to you."

"No, no, man. Don't blow me off. You don't understand. I need help *today, now,* not tomorrow or the day after."

"I'll see what I can do. I'll get back to you."

"No, you won't. You'll help me. *Now!* Get it? I've got enough on you to put you in San Quentin. Compree-hen-dee, aye-mee-goe? I can link you to every cheap heist in town."

"Jesus Christ, Damy, you wouldn't . . ."

"I will if I have to. Listen, man, I'm desperate. I'm going to cash in every brownie point I've got on you, all the favors you owe me. I need help and I need it now. Not tomorrow. I need a place to stash that fuckin' car! Compree-hen-dee?" Conde paused. "Hey, Conde, you still there?"

"Yeah. Damy, about all I can think of is my aunt's place. Jesus Christ, this is crazy. She's gone to Fresno to visit her sister. She's a little funny upstairs. Know what I mean?"

"So what?"

"She's going through some kind of religious thing."

"Like what?"

"A trauma or something. I don't know. Like rejecting all of her Catholic values. It's weird. She's always been such a devout Catholic. I'm not sure what's going on. She doesn't go to church anymore, and she keeps talking about the Devil."

Damy laughed. "Hell, I don't give a shit about that. As long as she's got a place where I can stash that car for a while. That's all I care about. Does she have a garage?"

"Yeah, she's got a garage she never uses. She never locks it. I went by her place yesterday. The garage is all cleaned out. It's immaculate. And, for some reason, she keeps the doors wide open."

"Perfect. Look, I want you to come and pick up the car."

"You want me to do *what?*"

"Pick up the car."

"Are you nuts?"

"Don't worry. I've changed the plates. Besides, they're looking for me, not you. Can you do that?"

"When?"

"Today."

"*Today?*"

"*Today.*"

"Jesus Christ, Damy, you're really muscling me."

"I know."

"You're really being chickenshit."

"Chill out, Conde. Just do it. And, hey?"

"What?"

"What's her name?"

"Who?"

"Your fruitcake aunt?"

"Tía Delfina."

"What?"

"Delfina Varela."

# 24. Germanic Fate

Fate watched Ruy Lopez, amused. Implacable Fate sat there like something out of a George Grosz 1926 painting: very German, very fat, bursting out of a gray suit, wearing a white shirt whose collar was so tight it made the veins in its neck bulge. Fate with its round, almost circular shoes on two small, fat feet. Sweating fate had just had a meal: several bratwurst sausages, potato pancakes, sauerkraut and six German beers, and now it sat there, a satisfied smile on its pink face. Every now and then Fate raised a hand full of thick, pink fingers to a pair of oily lips to suppress a belch. Fate, content and harmonious. Germanic Fate.

Fate sat there that day on Ruy's favorite easy chair. It was grinning, for it was about to present Ruy with a pair of remarkable ironies. The first portion was about to be served in the bedroom of Ruy's home. Fate could hardly contain its glee.

Ruy walked into his house to find everything in order. The bathrooms were sparkling and clean and smelled of Pine-Sol and even Lulusa had been washed. How strange, he thought, as he inspected a vacuumed rug, glistening windows, polished furniture. Ruy became suspicious of what all this cleanliness could mean. He walked into a dark bedroom and switched on the lights. There on the bed, sitting on his shirt —the beautiful striped one given to him by Alexis—was Amapola. She was also sitting on his tie—the one with the diagonal stripes, another present from Alexis, the one he would wear tonight on a date with her. Alexis was taking him to the San Francisco Ballet to see *Giselle.* A puzzled Ruy hardly knew what to make of Amapola's presence. She looked very contrite, very apologetic, very dark, needing, craving a beating, punishment for her indiscretions, her sins. She wanted to complete the Catholic cycle of sin, pleasure, remorse, repentance, punishment and absolution. Her chocolate eyes looked doleful and sad. She looked awful. She had gained weight and she looked shorter, fatter and darker, much darker. My God, she was dark, thought Ruy. What a contrast to Alexis with her slenderness, her fine bone-china hands, her alabaster neck.

Ruy felt very sorry for Amapola. Things had obviously not worked out between Amapola and Pelon. Ruy had hoped they could have worked something out. He had always imagined what this scene would be like: penitent wife, irate husband outraged, screaming. His favorite Hispanic scenarios were always being wasted. But he couldn't rise to anger now. The Hispanic melodrama was beginning to fade, becoming stale. It all seemed like part of the past, a Mexican past; part of a *machismo* ethic that in the end was destructive and self-defeating. Gone was the crushed pride. Missing was the outrage and the operatic ranting that Amapola was expecting, along with the smashed objects and the cursing. Instead there was Ruy very subdued and friendly. Alexis would soon arrive to take him to, of all things, the San Francisco Ballet.

And there too was Amapola sitting on his fine oxford-cloth shirt. Ironically, he wanted to embrace Amapola. She looked so forlorn, a kicked puppy. But, of course, that's exactly what she now sought: sympathy. It was part of the pose and he had to be very careful with her. There was a bit of balancing involved here now. Ruy had to be discreet. What to do with Amapola, who was sitting on his good shirt? It was all very polite, quite decent and civilized, almost English. Who could have asked for anything nicer? Ruy was the perfect gentleman. He got dressed in front of Amapola, discreetly turning his back to her when he slipped on his pants. In his coolness and lack of emotion, he almost resembled a *gabacho,* a white Anglo-Saxon Protestant.

"How have you been, Amy?" It sounded forced. Amy? He had never called her that before. "Can I get you some iced tea?" Since when did he start drinking iced tea? What happened to the brown quarts of Lucky Lager beer? Amapola sniffed the air. And since when did he start wearing cologne? Ruy had always considered cologne too effeminate, the perfume of *maricones.*

Amapola was disappointed. She had expected, sought even, a dramatic, emotional confrontation with an outraged bull. Instead here was this graceful, sleek animal looking thin and handsome wearing fancy loafers and smelling of cologne. He had even lost weight. He was being very cool to her. Cold even, and, worst of all, unresponsive. She wanted, she needed pain and yet all he gave her was indifference. On top of it all he was feeling sorry for her. She could feel it.

Ruy examined Amapola. In that harsh light, her skin, which had at one time looked smoky and exotic, now looked coarse and leathery. Her makeup was too light for her complexion, he thought. It only served to emphasize the darkness at her neck and arms. He wanted to step back, step away from her, disassociate himself from her darkness, her chipped fingernails, her dark rouge, her excessive eye makeup, which at one time he had liked. He thought of Alexis, and this woman before him seemed very distant now, a dead relative, foreign, a part of an unsubtle, emotional past he felt he had now outgrown. Amapola wiped her nose. Her eyes were tear-filled. And look at her, the poor dear, she wanted sympathy. She went to a chair, eased into it carefully and then sat up by propping herself forward awkwardly. Ruy shook his head. She was aching for pity. He had to resist the obvious urge to beat her or to console her. Instead he looked at his watch. Alexis and the night awaited.

"I really should get going, Amy."

Late that night, Ruy returned home and was surprised to find Amapola still up, still there. She had cleaned and waxed the floors and washed and ironed his laundry. Amapola stared at Ruy. He looked so handsome in his shirt and tie. Ruy poured two glasses of mineral water, offered one to Amapola, which she accepted, and then sat back in his favorite easy chair. Amapola sipped her drink.

"You're still up. It's late," said Ruy.

"I hope it's not too late," said Amapola. Ruy caught the irony and smiled, exhaling. Amapola detected Ruy's hesitancy, a bit of sadness. "What's the matter?"

"Nothing."

She knew him too well. "Something's happened. *¿Qué paso?*"

Ruy shook his head, sipped his drink. *"Nada."*

After a short silence, Amapola asked, "How's your new girl friend? I hear she's a real beauty." Ruy shook his head. "What's the matter?"

Ruy looked into his glass of mineral water. Finally, he spoke. "It's over, Amy."

Amapola corrected him. "Amapola."

"Amapola."

"What happened?"

"She goes back to school in Barcelona and tomorrow she begins a tour across Europe. It's the end of the summer. It's the end of the party."

"Well, can't you still see her, talk to her? There are airplanes and telephones."

Ruy shook his head again. "What for? These things never go on. It could never be the same. She's too young, too pretty. I've been a summer toy for her. Better to just let it drift away. I knew it would end, and yet when it does end . . ." Ruy swallowed.

To make him feel better, Amapola spoke up. "Well, Pelon left me too."

Ruy laughed and then remembered some of the things he liked about Amapola, her blunt honesty, her absolute lack of pretense. "We're both a couple of rejects," said Ruy.

Amapola went to him and he placed his arm around her waist and then eased her gently into his lap. "A pair of old, stinking sneakers that should go into the garbage can," said Amapola. Ruy began to laugh. He could feel the moisture in his eyes. "A pair of old, beat-up boots that even the garbage man won't take," said Amapola, placing her arms around Ruy's neck and leaning her head on his chest. They remained that way silently. Ruy sipped his drink. Finally, Amapola whispered, "No more booze?"

"No more booze."

"Why?"

"Why not?" Ruy had learned to answer a question with a question.

"Things have changed."

"A little."

"How's Molly?"

"O.K."

"And Lulusa?"

"As nasty as ever."

"I've missed you, Ruy."

"I've missed you too, Amapola."

Fate burped. It was feeling hungry again.

# 25. Politics III: Election Night

La Lunita Restaurant glowed with bright light, song and triumph that night. The outside of the restaurant was adorned with red, white and blue banners and three-foot-high posters of a smiling Victor Lopez. For Victor it was a critical night, election night, and he had chosen La Lunita, the site of so many political strategy meetings, as his election-night headquarters. He, Manny Caballos and Tony Bradlee occupied a large Naugahyde booth situated in front of an overhead television set that was turned on. As they watched the election returns, Manny and Victor sipped at margaritas made with José Cuervo tequila. Bradlee was drinking his usual Scotch.

Periodically, an explosion of light would bathe the booth in a bright, intense glare as a television camera and microphone would be thrust perilously close to Victor's face. "Realistically, Mr. Lopez, what *do* you think your chances are of beating von Meisterding tonight?"

"I not only think my chances are excellent, I know I'm going to win."

Victor had answered that question several times that day, and throughout the campaign, and would answer it several more times that night. As he was being interviewed he could see his own image appear on the television screen directly in front of him. Betraying his exhaustion, he appeared relaxed, personable, enthusiastic.

When the bright lights were turned off, when their eyes could focus back on the restaurant's dim interior, the Tecate beer posters, the bright *sarapes,* the murals, the Mexican sombreros, the three men could make out a shuffling figure.

An old man carrying a musical instrument ambled into La Lunita and began to play a sentimental Andalusian tune on a badly scuffed harp. He had so few teeth he was too embarrassed to smile and he played so poorly he no longer played for money, just sympathy and a possible drink. The restaurant owner rushed to the musician to eject him but Manny Caballos intervened. *"Déjalo.* I want to hear this," said Caballos. Seeing that his song was being appreciated by a political functionary, the old man straightened his stained jacket, stood erect, pursed his mouth and began to play proudly and with feeling, looking through the permanent tears in his eyes to a time when he was young and handsome and could play well. When he was through he rested the harp carefully by a wall, as if the splintering instrument were a priceless Baroque antique, and went over to Victor's table where Caballos palmed a bill into his hand. Without looking at the money, the old man looked into Caballos's eyes with a teary, genuine tenderness. He grinned toothlessly and spoke exuberantly about Seville, Córdoba and Granada, and no one could possibly understand one word of what he said.

Another incandescent flash of light, another microphone, another interview and the old man's image faded into the harsh glare of the television lights and disappeared.

"Are you optimistic tonight, Mr. Lopez?"

"Very."

"Why?"

"The latest polls show that I've caught up with Meisterding, and most pollsters are now saying the race is too close to call."

"Tell me, what accounted for your strong surge in the polls at the end of the campaign?"

"The reasons are sitting right here next to me, Tony Bradlee and Manny Caballos, two men who have been invaluable to the success of the campaign."

"How so?"

"Manny Caballos has been the monetary, the spiritual force behind the campaign; Tony Bradlee has been its driver. Tony has been unbelievable. He's put in long, hard hours and has helped convey our message of change and hope to everyone we've attempted to reach. Not only did he . . ."

But, of course, the reporter was uninterested in Manny Caballos or Tony Bradlee, and Victor's acknowledgments were cut short by another obvious, facile question.

"Tell me about your message of hope and change, Mr. Lopez."

The truth was Bradlee had thrown himself completely into Victor's campaign, enlisted every trick. To Victor's great benefit, Bradlee had cashed in every San Francisco political debt owed him. Bradlee had worked long, prodigious hours. Using the telephone, he was a master of persuasion. Bradlee had demanded and received political favors and contributions from his old political cronies. He, personally, had organized a sizable volunteer staff and had taken responsibility for the design and printing of all of Victor's campaign materials, including posters, which he even helped put up. Victor's fliers were everywhere to be seen: at supermarkets and shopping malls, at church bazaars and bingo parlors. Wherever more than six people had gathered in the Mission District, the chances were even that a volunteer had been there handing out Victor's leaflets.

Action committees had been formed for Mission District entrepreneurs and unions, businessmen and environmentalists, the young and the old, poor and rich, black and white, gay and straight. New mothers had received telephone calls congratulating them, as had anyone filing for a marriage license, a building permit or a business license. Personal notes had gone to anyone who donated as little as a dollar to Victor's campaign. Bradlee had even served as narrator for Victor's television and radio commercials. His gravelly voice—the result of countless packs of cigarettes and endless fifths of Scotch—had given Victor's television and radio commercials a deep, authoritarian ring. One could hardly turn away from Victor's commercials. It was as if the voice of God the Father Himself was vouching for Victor's political honesty, ordering, commanding, the listener to vote for Victor.

Bradlee also had a keen sense for the media. He had the professional journalist's instinct for news, and managed to get Victor at or near significant news events which garnered precious seconds of important evening news exposure and which eliminated the need for a costly advertising campaign.

"What about the charges made by von Meisterding's campaign coordinator, Conde Pacheco, that an expensive public relations and marketing firm has been involved in your campaign and that a secret, undeclared, political fund was created to help you?"

"That's a silly charge," replied Victor, "the false accusation of a desperate campaign. Conde Pacheco has tried to turn that accusation into a campaign issue and it's misfired for them. Badly. Voters can see through that obvious sham."

"I'm getting word now that some more returns are coming in, Mr. Lopez. Thank you."

"Thank *you.*"

The latest vote count appeared on the screen. It showed von Meisterding slightly ahead.

And there had been the speeches, the constant speeches. Victor had spoken before any group that would listen. He had attended coffee klatches and luncheons, high teas and afternoon barbecues, cocktail parties and dinners, perhaps all on the same day. He would speak all day and into the evening and when he was so exhausted that all he cared for was the comforting sight of his wife and sleeping baby daughter, Bradlee would make him appear at yet another community meeting or media interview where exactly the same questions had been repeated time and again. Bradlee had pushed Victor to the limit and then had pushed just a bit more.

Victor could hardly believe Bradlee's tenacity, his audacity, which, of course, paid off handsomely for Victor. His opinion of Bradlee had changed. He had not expected so much out of the dissipated, Scotch-drinking, cigarette-smoking, tread-worn political pro. Little wonder Bradlee had been so successful in the past.

"Mr. Bradlee, some people have accused you of having a personal political vengeance against von Meisterding. Is this true?"

Bradlee looked down at the lit cigarette in his fingers. For some reason there was a pitted black olive in the ashtray by his right hand. Bradlee took a long drag on the cigarette and stuck the glowing end into the olive, where it hissed out. "I have nothing against von Meisterding, or as they call him here, in the Mission District, 'Meester.' I do care about Victor, what he stands for, his campaign and his message of hope and change."

After countless political crusades Bradlee's response was glib and well rehearsed. After so many years of campaigning, his answers were so patented, so global, that any name could be inserted into the script; in this case it happened to be Victor's. Bradlee was like a traveling entertainer who had to look at a local matchbook cover to see where he had landed as he welcomed the local audience.

The truth was that Bradlee harbored no deep-seated animosity against von Meisterding. In fact, he hardly knew him except for what he had seen of Meester in his political ads or televised commercials. To him, Meester had been the opponent, the opposition, that gray adversary seen only in flickering shadows, the one he had challenged all of his life, the one he had to beat again, just one more time.

Caballos interjected. "Tony Bradlee is a professional. He works hard to defeat the opposition, whoever or whatever that may be." Caballos squeezed Bradlee's arm. "Why, this guy campaigns as if he has a year to live."

Caballos laughed. Victor laughed. Bradlee didn't. Not until later would Caballos realize the irony of his statement. For Bradlee had inoperable cancer and was given even less than a year to live. He had nothing to lose and he knew it and he had thrown himself recklessly into Victor's campaign, the last campaign of a dying pol.

"We've just received some more election results," said

the television reporter. "Let's go back to Sharon and Tony at Election Central."

A howl went off inside La Lunita Restaurant. The latest election tally showed Victor slightly ahead of Meester.

"Would you ever consider running for higher office, Mr. Lopez?"

Manny Caballos answered for him. "Of course. Someday Victor's going to be Governor of the State of California; maybe President of the United States of America!"

A resounding cheer went up in La Lunita Restaurant.

# 26. Delfina's Apparition

"Benjie told me he wants to stay here with me, Delfina."

"*Aiii,* Señora Talavera, Benjie tells you that every time I leave him here."

"Well, he likes it here. Cheap Thrills likes him. They never fight."

"He likes your cooking. He loves your *gallina en mole.*"

"*Cállate.* You know what else he likes?"

"What?"

"Melted Häagen-Dazs ice cream."

"*¿Deveras?*"

"*Sí.* He ate two quarts."

"*¿No me lo digas?*"

"How was Fresno and your dear sister, Chencha?"

"Terrible."

"Fresno or your sister?"

"Both."

"*¿Por qué?*"

"Well, Chencha was very sick from the chingles and, you know, crabby, and my *juanetes* bother me so much it hurts me to walk. I don't think I can take one more long trip."

*"Aiii, pobrecita."* Turning to see Benjie entering the room like a fat lion in a musical comedy, Señora Talavera recited a fast chorus of Spanish baby talk in a high, shrill voice *"Aiii, mira-nomas-quien entro: mi chulito, mi chiquitito, tan consentido, tan precioso, mi borreguito santísimo. Mira nomas, qué hermosura de gatito."*

With that kind of praise and adulation—plus the chicken in *mole* sauce, not to mention the two quarts of melted Häagen-Dazs ice cream—little wonder Benjie preferred to stay. Benjie went over by Señora Talaveras's ankles and flopped down with a thud.

*"Aiii,* you are spoiling him."

"He is already spoiled rotten, Delfina."

Delfina pulled up the sleeve of her black sweater to look at her watch, a Swatch watch with a pink wristband. She brought the watch up close to her face and then pulled it back to focus on it. *"Aiii, mira,* look at the time. I have to go." Delfina reached into a shopping bag and pulled out a thick, plastic mechanical pencil, which she gave to Señora Talavera proudly. On the clip of the pencil was a plastic garlic; the side of the pen bore the words "Gilroy: The Garlic Capital of the World."

*"Aiii, mira. Qué precioso,"* said Señora Talavera.

"Oh, it's nothing. *Nomas una mierdita.* A little something from Benjie for taking such good care of him."

"It is beautiful. *Gracias."*

*"De nada. Gracias a ti.* Well, I have to go."

Señora Talavera picked up Benjie and handed him to Delfina. As she picked up the cat it passed a small amount of gas.

*"Aiii, Chihuahua,"* said Delfina. "He is getting *so* fat."

"Yes, but he is so *chulo*," said Señora Talavera, petting the cat before lapsing back into baby talk. *"Mira nomas, tan fallón, tan precioso."* Smelling the cat's offering, she added, *"Tan apestosito."*

*"A Dios."*

*"A Dios."*

Delfina walked away from Señora Talavera's house carrying a shopping bag in one hand and Benjie in the other. The cat was so stupefied from eating that it draped itself listlessly over Delfina's arm, where it hung like a dead, fat chicken, its eyes glazed over.

Delfina was glad to have seen her sister in Fresno but gladder to be back in the Mission District with all of its hubbub and familiar smells and sights. The smell of *carnitas* aroused Benjie, who licked his chops. The cat, who now weighed twenty-one pounds, hadn't been fed in thirty-seven minutes. Benjie made a face, as if he was about to encounter something malodorous. Approaching them were Señorita Dolores and Señorita Lucrecia.

*"Buenos días,* Delfina," said Señorita Lucrecia.

*"Buenos días,"* said Delfina curtly.

"How is Benjie?" said Señorita Dolores, pointing to the semicomatose cat.

"Fine."

"He is getting big. You don't think you are feeding him too much, do you?"

"No. He comes from a family of big cats."

"Well, he looks fat to me."

"Have you been away, Delfina?" asked Señorita Dolores innocently.

That was the last straw. First they condemn her precious

Benjie and now this. Silly snoops, thought Delfina. They knew perfectly well she had been away. "I went to Hollywood to make a movie with Anthony Quinn," snapped Delfina, turning and walking away smartly. Benjie purred his approval.

"*Mira nomas*," said Señorita Lucrecia.

"*Qué grosera*," said Señorita Dolores.

"*Santa Delfina.*"

"*La Gran Reina Delfina.*"

"*Maldita sea.*"

Delfina passed a lunch wagon whose sides proclaimed, "Beto's Lonch Vagon of Savory Treets." Someone had deleted the letter "r" from the word "treets" with a spray can.

Delfina passed a bar that smelled of urine, a laundromat where a bald-headed Asian man kept staring at a dryer door to see his tumbling laundry, an auto shop where a power tool was removing bolts and a school whose outer wall depicted members of different races marching arm in arm toward a sunrise and a new day. Finally she turned into Ortigalita Street to be greeted by a familiar, pleasing sight: her own small, two-story Victorian house with its cascade of bougainvillea flowers.

Delfina was puzzled. "There is something different, Benjie. Something has changed."

Delfina put down her shopping bag and shifted Benjie to her right arm like a drooping sack of potatoes as she inspected the items on her front porch: the pot of plastic flowers in a green flowerpot shaped like a fish, the junk mail sticking out of the mail slot in her front door, the green welcome mat that bore two frogs sitting on a water lily plant next to the words

"Welcome to my pad." The bougainvillea had lost some leaves but that was to be expected.

And then she remembered. She had left the garage door open to receive her car. The door was now closed! And her lovely, hand-painted sign was missing. The one that warned,

NO PARKING EVER
THIS MEANS YOU MISTER
YOU WILL BE SORRY

Probably the work of those naughty neighborhood boys, she thought; the same ones who tipped over her garbage cans on Tuesdays when the trash was picked up, the ones who brought their dogs over to poop on her walkway. *"Malditos sean."*

She went to open the garage door. Delfina felt a slight chill of panic. *"¡Ave María Purísima!"* The door was locked! From the *inside!*

*"¡Qué raro!* This is strange, Benjie, very strange." Benjie meowed. Delfina was gripping him tightly. "It is a sign, a sign from . . . from . . . It is a sign."

Delfina went around to a side window. The little black curtain she had fashioned was slightly askew. Shading her eyes from the reflection in the window, she peeked into the garage. There was something inside. She squinted, wiped the window with her sleeve and then peeked in again. She could make something out. It was . . . it was . . . Now she could make it out! It was shiny and red.

It was an apparition!

*"¡Es mi carro!"*

She stepped back, startled, dropping Benjie into a flower bed, where he landed with a thud. *"¡Madre Santísima!"* Delfina was suddenly frightened. "It is the car. The Devil has brought me my car!" And then the realization struck her; she could hardly contain her glee. With a limp that favored her left foot, Delfina rushed to open her front door, stepping over a stack of junk mail and bills. She wanted to share her joy and immediately telephoned her sister. "I have some wonderful news, Chencha. You will not believe what has just happened to me. No, I have not won the Lotto. It is even better. When I got home . . . *Aiii, mira,* I am so excited. When I got home . . . *Aiii, mira,* I will have to call you back, Chencha. I am too nervous to talk. *Es el carro del Diablo."*

Delfina hung up and Chencha in Fresno, who, through her illness, had been subjected to her sister's preposterous tales about Catholicism and the Devil for the past three days, shook her head, made the sign of the cross and rolled over in bed.

Delfina was so happy she could cry as she went into the garage to inspect her car. She unlocked the garage door and watched it swing up as a spring growled and slapped the door open. In the direct sunlight, Delfina looked at her new car, petting the hood, the fenders, the doors.

"It is *so* pretty," said Delfina, and Benjie agreed. The colors were red and black, the colors of fire and charcoal. Delfina nodded. "The colors of the Devil," she announced proudly. "Just wait until Dolores and Lucrecia see this."

She inspected the car carefully, opened a door, sat behind the wheel and touched the dashboard, the leather seats, the gearshift. The car seemed small. "If I get another person in here, where am I going to put the groceries, Benjie?" Benjie agreed.

She looked at the odometer. "But this car is not new," she told Benjie. And then she ran her fingers over the name of the car: C-o-r-v-e-t-t-e. *"Corbette? Ya que.* That is not the way you spell *Cadiyác."* Benjie growled. What kind of a name was that? What kind of a car was that? She wanted a *Cadiyác,* not a, a whatchamacallit, a *Corbette.* She closed the car door gently and went inside the house to make a telephone call. Delfina called a car dealer and was saddened to learn the news.

"You mean a Corbette is nothing but a *Cheeby!"* Delfina exclaimed. "A Che-bro-lett?"

"That's right, ma'am, a Chevrolet product."

*"Ah, vaya."* Delfina could hardly hide her distress.

"I know what you're thinking, ma'am. You're terribly disappointed, aren't you, ma'am? You know, you'd be much better off with a Chrysler Imperial, ma'am. That's a classy little car. This week we're having a special on a slightly used Chrysler Imperial. It was driven by a little old Mexican lady, just like yourself. It's a cream puff, a real cherry."

"Excuse me?"

"Oh, sorry, ma'am. I mean it's a real honey of a car and we're ready to make you a real honey of a deal. You belong in a Chrysler Imperial, ma'am. We'll take that dog of a Corvette off your hands, use it for a trade-in and take care of all the financing for you, ma'am. After all, Santos Brothers is the 'Home of the Iddy-Biddy Better Deal.'"

"I know all about the little deals made by the Santos

Brothers," said Delfina, laying the receiver in its cradle very slowly.

"Ma'am? Ma'am? Don't . . ." The car salesman was sinking into oblivion. "Ma'am, don't hang up on . . ."

Delfina hung up on the car salesman and stared sadly at the telephone until she realized it was ringing.

"¿Ola?"

"Ma'am? Is this Miss Delfeena Barrel?"

"Delfina Varela."

"Right. Hi, this is DuWayne Tull. You just called, ma'am, about dumping a Corvette and looking at the great deal we're offering on a slightly used Chrysler Imperial?"

Delfina began to lay the receiver back into its cradle a second time.

"Ma'am, ma'am, don't hang up on me. Shit! Goddamn it! Don't!"

Delfina hung up on the car salesman and unplugged the telephone. She couldn't believe the depth of her disappointment. She had ended up with a Chevrolet, and worst of all a *used* Chevrolet. *"Mierda,"* said Delfina, and Benjie fully agreed. "A stinking *Corbette.*" Her disappointment turned to resignation. "But I guess in my heart I always knew it would be a *Cheeby. Ya que.* At my age. When you're a *viejita* you have to be thankful for whatever you can get. What did I expect? *Ya que. Algo es mejor que nada.*"

That night, a siren interrupted Delfina's splendid dream of stars, a full moon and a handsome, 1950s Anthony Quinn driving her in her car along the California coast on their way down to Santa Barbara and ecstasy.

"Is that too windy for you and Benjie, Delfina, *querida?*"

asked Anthony Quinn as in her dream he reached over to squeeze her hand and then to pet Benjie, who sat in her lap.

"No, Toño, tha's O.K., *mijito*," replied Delfina as she adjusted a sailboat-motif Hermes scarf around her neck.

"With that scarf, in this moonlight, you look so beautiful, Delfina. It makes you look like Dolores Del Rio."

"*Aiii,* Toño, you probably say that to all the girls."

"None as beautiful as you, *preciosa.*"

The siren got louder, closer. The Hermes scarf, Anthony Quinn and the moonlit coastal drive evaporated as Delfina sat up in her bed. Her hand seemed to be warm from the touch of Anthony Quinn's hand. She could hear a car slide to a stop in front of the house and then drive off, its tires squealing. Someone had run out of the car. The next sound she heard was her garage door slamming shut just as two police cars sped by, their sirens wailing.

"*Ave María Purísima,*" said Delfina, putting on a flowery nightgown. She could hear the door leading from the garage to her kitchen being thrown open and then someone opening a faucet and drinking water in loud slurps.

Delfina hobbled into the living room to turn on a lamp and found herself standing face-to-face with a young, blond man in a black leather jacket aiming a 9mm pistol directly at her face.

It was Damy Taggart.

# El Diablo

Was it really him: the Prince of Darkness?

# 27. The Devil, Delfina Varela and an Empyrean Wound

*Ave María Purísima!*"

Delfina Varela thought the Devil would be ugly. He was so handsome and young and he had blond hair and a beard just like in the Holy Picture Cards of Jesus as a young man. No wonder people liked the Devil so much. *¡Qué guapo!* He was *so* good looking. And he wore Devil clothes too: baggy pants, black athletic shoes and a black leather jacket. Was it really him: the Prince of Darkness?

"It is *you*. *¿Verdad, Demonio?*"

"What in the fuck are you talking about?" asked Damy. "Make a move and I'll blow your brains out." Delfina smiled. It *was* the Devil. It *had* to be. Besides she always knew the Devil would speak that way, direct and to the point, dirty. English. "What the fuck are you talking about?" Devils spoke English and used the word "fuck" a lot. Fuck, fuckin', fucking; fuckie-fuck-fuck.

"You brought me the car. ¿*Verdad?* And now you want to take my immortal soul. ¿*Verdad, Demonio?*"

"Holy shit! I heard you were wacko but this is . . ." Taggart grimaced, lowered the pistol. "You are . . ."

"Delfina Varela." He was probably checking to make sure he had the right address, thought Delfina; like Santa Claus, he probably had a lot of stops to make.

Taggart started to talk and then dropped to both knees. Delfina was flattered that the sound of her name should bring such veneration. Taggart touched his right side with his left hand and then crawled to lie down on a living room sofa. When he turned, his jacket pulled aside to reveal a crisp white linen shirt. Almost the entire right side of it was shining with flowing blood. Delfina approached Taggart. *"Ave María Purísima.* I will get some help, *Demonio."*

"No, no, don't." The Devil was in pain. "Call the police or a doctor and I'll blow your face off," he said, pointing the gun at an awkward angle at Delfina and then lowering it. He grimaced.

"Yes, *Demonio.*"

"Why do you keep calling me . . ."

Before he could finish, Taggart turned to lie back on the sofa, dropping his head to one side. Blood was seeping from his shirt.

"You live alone. Right?"

"Not right."

"Who else lives here?"

"Benjie."

"Who's that?"

"My *gatito.*"

"Your what?"

"My keetie-cat."

Taggart closed his eyes and ran his fingers through his greasy hair. "This is wonderful . . . I nearly get my guts blown out and I end up with . . . this first-water fruitcake who lives here with her keetie-cat named . . . Benjie . . ." Taggart tried to laugh but began to choke. He was breathing hard as he hesitated, tried to raise himself and then fell back, dropping the gun at Delfina's feet before sinking into a delirious sleep.

Delfina examined the gun with curiosity. She had never seen a real gun before, only in museums or on the TV or in the movies at the Tower Theater. She touched the gun, picked it up. It was cold and heavy. She was thrilled. She had not felt like that since the first time she had touched Panchito, her late husband, on his manhood.

Delfina placed the gun on a doily and went to the window to see two police cars racing up Ortigalita Street, their sirens wailing, their red lights flashing. Delfina was almost breathless. Her prayers to *El Diablo* had finally been answered.

Delfina removed Taggart's clothes with great difficulty as he groaned. She was able to take off his shoes and pants and ended up tearing away most of his shirt, which was shredded with tiny holes. She cleaned the blood off of his body with a damp towel to reveal a frightening wound on the right side of his chest. When she came too close to the wound, Taggart, by now perspiring, moaned, his eyes closed, "Oh, oh no. Please. Please don't . . ." before passing out again. As she cleaned and bandaged the ghastly wound all she could think of was that he had probably received it in a celestial battle with St. Michael the Archangel. The two never *did* learn to get along. When she had washed him, she wrapped him in gauze and bandages, from neck to belly button, from chest to back, and then covered him with a sheet and a blanket and propped his perspiring head on a pillow, where he slept soundly for hours.

That afternoon, Delfina returned with her two-wheeled shopping cart filled with groceries. The nosy checkout clerk, seeing all of the food in her basket, had asked, "My, Delfina, you must be having a party. Will there be lots of cute, young boys?"

"One hundred. It is none of your business what I buy. This is a free country," Delfina had replied. Nosy people. As if she could tell the little snoop that the food was for the Devil. Sure, tell the checkout girl *El Demonio* was staying with her and right away she would tell Señorita Dolores or Señorita Lucrecia and before you knew it they would be interviewing her on the TV about the Devil's favorite food and the color of his underwear—which happened to be red, incidentally.

She found Taggart lying peacefully on her living room sofa. The sun, filtered by an undulating lace curtain, was laying a dappled pattern of swirling light across his nude body. He was no longer perspiring. He had thrown the covers on the floor and lay stretched out, completely naked except for a Rolex watch, two diamond rings on his fingers and the large bandages across his chest and rib cage. What a beautiful body, thought Delfina. She examined him carefully. He was *so* good looking. She had not seen a man's naked body in years, not since Panchito died. But even that was different. This body was young and slender and smooth. Panchito's was fat, dark and hairy. She inspected his beard, the blond hair on the Devil's chest, his blond pubic hair, his penis, whose foreskinned tip pointed at his thigh. She wondered how many women had felt the fury and pleasure of that now-recumbent member. It was the first time in eight years she had seen a man's penis. He was so much bigger than dear Panchito. In the old days, before she hooked up with the Devil, she would have said, *"Ave María Purísima,"* or at the very least made the sign of the cross touching a crossed thumb and index finger to her forehead, stomach and left and right shoulders. But that was before, before the arrival in her house of the Devil, who had brought her the car. And then she looked at the automatic pistol on the end table. She couldn't decide which held more awe for her. To Delfina both symbolized great power and great terror: the dull gray pistol with its dark wooden handle and that pink penis, which now looked as sweet and innocent as a sleeping baby. When would either be used in the heat of passion again? she wondered. She placed the sheet and blanket across Taggart, covering him as he groaned and turned slightly, his hand instinctively reaching for the pistol.

Delfina went over to Taggart and whispered, "Devil, when are you going to let me drive the car?"

Taggart's eyes opened slightly. They appeared to be glazed. He said something softly, almost tenderly.

*"¿Cómo?"* asked Delfina, bringing her ear close to Taggart's lips.

What she heard was a very slow, very belabored whisper. "You. Wacko. Bitch. What. Is. The. Matter. With. You." Taggart turned away from his wounds and sank back into a deep sleep.

# 28. Politics IV: The Election Results and the Unquenchable Dream

Manny Caballos, Victor Lopez and Tony Bradlee had ordered breakfast at La Lunita Restaurant: *huevos rancheros,* coffee and bread rolls called *bolillos.* Caballos and Victor looked down and picked at their food like children forced to eat Brussels sprouts. Only Bradlee ate heartily of the egg, chile and tortilla dish.

"Sons-of-bitches!" Caballos was animated, livid. "It was Conde Pacheco. He's responsible. To think that a Chicano would screw us over."

Victor Lopez pushed his plate away and attempted to assuage the older man. "That had nothing to do with it, Manny. Conde Pacheco is Conde Pacheco. Besides, it's not the end."

"Bullshit! Give up on this one and then the next one and

the one after that. Bow your head like a beaten little Mexican *campesino* and say, '*Sí, señor, vuestra merced.* It is your land; it is your country. It is the Will of God.' Bullshit! I'm going to fight."

Tony Bradlee sipped at his coffee and snapped open a Zippo lighter, lit a cigarette and took a long drag. "Fight what, Manny? Thin air? It's over."

"Never."

"At least for this round. Your dream has to be postponed for a little while, at least," said Bradlee, the cigarette dangling from his mouth.

"But we haven't lost yet," insisted Caballos.

"Yes, we have," rebutted Bradlee, speaking through a haze of smoke that twisted across his face. "Time for Victor to make a sweet speech conceding the election. The way you leave this campaign will pave the way for the next one. It's what people remember."

Caballos insisted. "But what about the two hundred write-in votes that were 'mysteriously' lost and then 'mysteriously' found again, all favoring Meester? You can't tell me that somebody didn't buy *somebody*."

"You can't prove a damn thing, Manny," pleaded Victor. "We've already gotten a recount and the results still show Meester winning by a hundred twenty-six votes."

"A hundred twenty-six votes, my ass!" fumed Caballos. "I want to see the ballots. I want to sue."

"You don't have a leg, Manny." The political pro spoke from experience. "In the end you'll lose. You'll lose time, patience and money; all to get something off your chest. It's not worth it. Save all three for the next campaign. There will always be the next campaign."

Victor thought it interesting that Bradlee always spoke of campaigns, not elections.

"But it's so unfair," Caballos pleaded.

"Manny, fairness is irrelevant; it's called politics, and politics has nothing to do with justice," said Bradlee, stubbing out his cigarette in a mound of refried beans.

Victor acknowledged Meester's victory in a speech that was generous and conciliatory. Bathed again in the glare of television lights, Victor appeared poised and articulate as he thanked his supporters and volunteers and a long list of individuals including his own brother, Ruy Lopez.

Manny Caballos looked at the reporters and shook his head. Bradlee was probably right. The way you left this campaign paved the way for the next one. "It's what people remember." And, by God, there *would* be a next time. Caballos stared at Victor, who looked so proud, so handsome. It took very little to trigger Manny Caballos's favorite fantasy. Perhaps someday there *could* be a Mexican in the White House, a Mexican-American President of the United States of America; someone with great poise and wit; a Mexican John F. Kennedy with a bristling moustache. Caballos smiled and looked east, toward Washington, into the future.

# 29. The Devil Recuperates

Delfina Varela harbored Damy Taggart through his delirious convalescence giving him honey and lemon tea and Mexican penicillin—*albóndiga* and *pozole* soups—while subjecting him to those wonderful Spanish-language soap operas, *Manuela* and *Simplemente María*.

Perhaps it was time to put away the crucifix that glowed in the dark, also the picture of the Sacred Heart of Jesus. This was probably what was making the Devil so sick, thought Delfina. That and all the little holes in his side that were put there by St. Michael the Archangel. She removed the crucifix to a back closet and turned the picture of the Sacred Heart of Jesus so that the Devil could not see it, so that the Devil could get well.

Miraculously, it worked.

To complete the healing process, Delfina bought Damy a bedpan and tried to persuade him to take an enema or a laxative.

"It will be good for you," she said, holding up an enema bag with its trailing hose and nozzle.

"What's that?"

"It's a—I don't know how you call it in English—in Spanish it is called a *lavativa*. It is good for you."

"What's it for?"

"Well, see this," said Delfina, holding up a long nozzle. "You put this inside of you from the bottom and then . . ."

"Shit, it's a goddamn enema bag. Get that thing out of my face."

"It will clean out the poisons in your body."

"Stick it up your own butt."

Delfina relented. He sounded so upset she wouldn't force him to take an enema. That was too bad; an enema would probably cure him. A good enema consisted of warm water, salt and ground jalapeño pepper seeds. That was the very best. Perhaps she could slip a little laxative into his soup.

That's how she could tell that he was *really* the Devil. No good Catholic would possibly refuse to take enemas or laxatives. For some reason all she could think of when she thought of laxatives or enemas was Señorita Lucrecia and Señorita Dolores. God, if only Lucrecia or Dolores could see her now. But, of course, she couldn't tell a soul. Those two would blab it all over the world and she could very well lose her car.

That night Taggart awoke her. "Delfina!" He was getting louder. He was getting better. She had been watching television and had dozed off. He was yelling at her. "Goddamn, can't you hear me? Bring me a pair of scissors and a mirror. I want to trim my beard."

"*Sí, Demonio,*" said Delfina.

"Why do you keep *calling* me that? Why don't you call me by my first name?"

"What is your name?"

"Damy."

"Damy? What kind of a name is that? That is the name for a woman; or a little boy."

"My full name's Damien."

Delfina smiled. "Of course." *Demonio* was another name for *Diablo.*

"Hell, call me whatever pops into your simple pea brain. What do I care?" Taggart attempted to rise but fell back. "Cripes." He stared at Delfina.

"What is the matter?"

"Look, I want you to do something for me."

"Chure. You are the boss."

"In the car behind the driver's seat, there's a small storage box. You open it by pressing a button. Do you understand what I'm saying?"

"Chure. In my car behind the driver's seat, there is a small box. I open it by pressing a little button."

"Good. You're not as dumb as you look."

"I am not the one with the little holes in my side from St. Michael."

"Jesus Christ! Now what are you talking about? When you open the storage unit . . . Are you listening?"

"Yep."

"When you open the storage unit there's a false panel underneath that. You've got to open it with a Phillips screwdriver. Do you know what that is?"

"Nope."

"That's a screwdriver with a tip that looks like a little cross. Sort of like this." Taggart crossed two fingers.

Delfina knew exactly what the Devil meant. "You mean like the roof of St. Mary's Cathedral."

"Yeah, that's it."

The roof of St. Mary's Cathedral was constructed in the shape of a horizontal cross with tapering sides. She could see St. Mary's every time she looked up Valencia Street.

"Ah, *sí.*"

"Do you have one of those?"

"I *have* two."

"You have to what?"

"I have two of the leetle screwdrivers."

"Well, get the leetle screwdriver, open the leetle storage compartment, undo the leetle Phillips screws, lift the leetle panel and bring me the case that's inside. Compree-hen-day?"

"*¿Cómo?*"

"Do you understand?"

"Yes, but not your terrible Spanish."

"Well, chop-chop. Get going. Don't just stand there."

As Delfina labored to open the car panel, she could hear Taggart talking on the telephone. It sounded like he was talking to a woman. "Baby, I know it's late, but I need a *big* favor . . ." He was probably going about his business, getting ready to seduce some more women, she thought.

After almost an hour, Delfina returned with Damy's attaché case, which he grabbed.

"Christ, it took you long enough."

"Well, the light in the garage is not too good and my eyes are not as good as from before."

A snapping sound was created by two spring latches which flipped up. Inside the case were two rows of plastic bags which held a white powder.

"*¿Qué es eso?*"

"Huh?"

"What is that?"

"What does it look like? Talcum powder to put on a baby's fanny. I want you to do me a big favor. Do you think you can do it?"

"How do I know if I think I can do it if I do not know the thing it is you want done?"

"I want you to deliver this stuff for me."

"What?"

"I want you to deliver this stuff."

"When?"

"Right now."

"*¿Qué cosa?* It is too late."

"Look, if I give you an address, do you think you can deliver this stuff for me?"

"Right now? The baby can wait."

"What?"

"The baby that needs the talcum powder for his bottom can wait."

"I'll make it worth your while."

"You mean you want me to take this to somebody right now?"

"No, a week, two weeks from tomorrow. Of course I want you to do it now."

"But it is pretty late. *Mira.* She put her wrist out to show Damy her pretty Swatch watch, the one with the pink strap.

"I don't care what time it is. Just do it. O.K.?"

"Well, I don' know. Maybe I could get lost. Maybe if I could get to drive my car."

"It's *not* your car. Look, deliver this stuff and I'll make it

worth your while. Believe me. Maybe I'll even let you drive
the car. O.K.? Now go get me a shopping bag. And some
paper and a pencil. Come on. Don't just stand there."

When Delfina returned with a shopping bag Taggart
placed all of the plastic bags inside the shopping bag along
with a handwritten note.

"This is going to be perfect," Damy said. "Who would
ever suspect a little old lady? Here, let me put this pillowcase
on top of the stuff. Perfect. Now, look, here's the address. Do
you think you can find it?"

Delfina peered at the note, stretched her arm out to focus
on the address. *"Aiii, Chihuahua."*

"What's the matter?"

"You have terrible handwriting. What does this say?"

"It's an address on Thirty-sixth Avenue."

*";Aiii, chispas!"*

"Now what?"

"The address. It would be easier to go to Fresno and it is
so late the buses are not running." Delfina studied the address
on the note. "That is not too close. It is on the other side of
San Francisco. I will have to take a bus and then another bus,
and my *juanetes* give me so much pain that . . ."

"I don't know what you're talking about," said Taggart
impatiently. "Look, just take a taxi."

"A taxi?" Delfina was shocked. To her taxis were an incredible luxury, something for the rich and important. "A
taxi? *Ya que.* I am not the President of the United States of
America. I do not have . . ."

"Look, don't worry. Here, take fifty bucks, make it a
hundred."

*Hijo 'e la,* thought Delfina. He *has* to be the Devil. He

pulls out the Big Stuff like it was a little dime and a quarter. Delfina went to the telephone.

"Oh, Christ, *now* what are you doing?"

"I am calling for a taxi like you said."

"Not from here, stupid. Don't call for a taxi from *here*. Call one from a telephone booth. Do you understand what I'm saying?"

"Of course. I am not stupid."

"Whatever the woman gives you when you deliver the stuff, have her place it in this same shopping bag. Have the taxi driver wait and then return in the same cab. Don't have him drop you off in front of this house. Get out two blocks away from here."

"Why should I take a taxi and then have to walk? My *juanetes* will . . ."

"Look. Just deliver the stuff and bring back what the woman gives you. Can you do that?"

"Only if you let me drive my car."

"Goddamn it, you sound like a broken record. When you get back maybe I'll let you drive the car, O.K.?"

"It is not O.K. 'Maybe' is *mierda.*"

"Look. I'll *give* you the damn car. Understand? How's that? I'll *give* it to you. But you've got to run the errand first."

"Now you are talking the good English."

# 30. The Realization of the Dream

When Delfina returned, Taggart grabbed the shopping bag out of her hand.

"Jesus Christ! It took you long enough. It's almost midnight. What the hell took you so long?"

"Well, the taxi guy could not find the address because it was so dark and he kept cussing, just like you, and then he did not wait for me, that *grosero*, so I call and wait for another taxi and then when I got back here I got, you know, lost. Just a leetle bit. It was pretty dark, you know, and then in the dark my *juanetes* . . . How about my car?"

Damy looked inside the shopping bag. "Why, you sweet, sweet old withered piece of poon tang."

"*¿Qué?* That sounds like a Chinese . . ."

"Goddamn! *God*-damn!" Damy looked up to the ceiling and held up the shopping bag. "I can't believe it. It worked! It actually worked. It's all here. Look at this." Damy waved several packets of tightly wrapped hundred-dollar bills at Delfina.

"*¡Socorro!*" Delfina had never seen so much money in her life.

Damy hugged several bundles of money to his chest. When he touched his wound he winced. "Ooooo. Damn!"

"*Demonio*, why don't you let me fix you a nice bowl of *pozole?* It will help you get well."

"I'm tired of your dumb soups and honey and lemon tea. I want to get the hell out of here."

What a funny expression for the Devil to use, thought Delfina. And then back to her prime concern. "When can I drive my car?"

Damy looked Delfina in the eye and said, "You want my car so bad you can taste it." Delfina noted that he was still calling it *his* car. "Don't you? Don't you, you crazy, dingy old bag? You want my car in the worst way. Don't you?"

Damy pinched Delfina's cheek.

"Ouchie!"

"And you want to know something?"

Delfina pouted. "I want *you* to know something. I want you to know that my cheek hurts. It is not funny. I do the errand for you like a servant and you pinch me hard on the cheek and call me a Chinese name and you said I could drive my car."

"You want to know something? Do you really want to know something, you crazy old fruit? I'm going to let you *have* that car. I'm actually going to *give* you that fuckin' car."

"It *is* my car. It is about time."

"I can't drive that thing anyway. Right now every cop in San Francisco is looking for it. They all want to become heroes and plug me driving it. What do I want with it? Look at this. More money than I could ever spend. I'm set for life. And you think I'm worried about that stupid car. I'm going to buy dozens of cars, hundreds of them. You know that? You don't even know what I'm talking about, do you?"

Delfina shrugged.

"Besides, you did pull it off. You dumb old fruitcake. You pulled me through all this; you also made that delivery." Damy patted Delfina on the cheek and shook his head; a new thought, a passing smile. "Wouldn't that be a bitch? The cops tracing that car to a dingy little old Mexican lady like you? That would actually be a gas." Damy Taggart laughed as he pulled some papers from the attaché case. "I'm going to do it. What the hell. It's my car; I can do whatever I want with it. Bring me a pen."

"You are upsetting Benjie."

"What's his problem?"

"You didn't say the magic word."

Frustrated, Taggart asked, "What are you talking about *now?*"

"The magic word. You didn't say it."

"What's the magic word?"

" 'Please.' "

"Sheeet." Taggart laughed. "O.K. Please."

"Thank you." Delfina went to the kitchen and returned with a pink pen that bore the name and telephone number of the Santos Brothers, "Home of the Iddy-Biddy Better Deal."

"Do you see what this is?" asked Taggart, waving an official-looking document.

"Of course. It is a piece of paper."

"Sheeet. It's the title for the car. I'm going to sign it over to you. Do you understand what I'm saying? Do you even understand what I'm doing?"

"*Claro.*"

"Can you read what it says here?"

"Of course." Delfina squinted at the paper that looked like a green bond certificate. She raised her head and held the paper at arm's length. She tilted her head to the right and then to the left. "What does it say?"

"Shit, you screwball. It says 'State of California. Certificate of Title.' Can't you see that?"

"Of course, I am not blind."

"I'm going to fill this out for you and sign it. Do you understand what I'm doing?"

"*Seguro.*"

"What's the address of this rat hole?"

"It is not a rat hole. It is my home. I have many happy mementos here. I have lived here most of my life. Panchito could make me happy when he wanted. You do not call it a . . ."

"O.K., O.K. What's the address?"

"850 Ortigalita."

"How do you spell that?"

"Oh, erre, te, ee, hay, ah, ele, ee, te, ah."

"Good God. Just show me an envelope with your address on it."

Delfina brought over a letter from her sister, Chencha.

"Who's this?"

"My sister in Fresno. She got the chingles."

"Thanks. O.K. 850 Ortigalita. San Francisco. California and your ZIP code. Date of sale is today. Purchase price is one dollar."

Delfina was shocked. "One dollar? I cannot tell people my car is only worth one dollar."

"Look, stupid, you're getting a brand-new Corvette for a dollar. Don't you understand a goddamn thing? Do you have a dollar?"

Delfina got her purse and turned her back to prevent *El Demonio* from inspecting its contents. "I have a leetle change. *Uno, dos, tres, cuatro.* I got four quarters."

"Look, just fill in the form. I'll do it for you." Delfina zippered her handbag shut and shoved it out of sight. "Here, come here. You've got to sign on this line."

Delfina refused. "I want to know what I am signing." Delfina was certain it was a certificate that would condemn her to Hell for all eternity in exchange for the car that was only worth one dollar. "My soul is worth more than one dollar."

"Oh, my God! Look, I'm *giving* you that fuckin' car. Don't you understand? Just, just sign this if you want the car, O.K.? Not there, stupid, over here. Here, I'll fill out the back for you before you screw everything up. There now. You—you dizzy bag—are now the proud owner of a new Corvette."

"O.K."

"You're the new registered owner. The car's yours. Understand?"

"*Gracias.*"

"Here, take this. You'll have to send that to Sacramento."

Delfina corrected Taggart's pronunciation. "*Sacramento.*"

"And here, take the car keys."

Delfina's face broke into a bright smile. The keys felt heavy and cold in her fingers. The transaction became real to her for the very first time. She felt as if she had just been handed the keys to the Gates of Heaven. But, of course, that was impossible. What the heck would the Devil be doing with the keys to the Pearly Gates of Heaven?

"I knew it would happen, *Demonio.* Oh, *Demonio,* you make me so happy. I have not been so happy since I married Panchito. Do you mind if I show these to Benjie?"

"*Jesus* Christ! Show them to the ants in your kitchen for all I care. The cockroaches."

"Here, Benjie, my baby. See what I got you? I told you I would get a car, *precioso.*" She picked up the cat and hugged it.

The telephone rang. Damy and Delfina looked at each other. Delfina shrugged and dropped the cat with a thud. Damy drew his pistol. "Answer that."

"*Ola.*"

"Hi, *tía?*"

"Who is this?"

"Conde, your nephew. How are you?"

"Why are you calling here, *ratero?*" Delfina looked at her watch. "At this hour? You never called me in your whole life."

"Let me talk to Damy."

"You mean *El Demonio,* Conde."

"Is that Conde?" said Damy, grabbing the telephone out of Delfina's hand.

"Hey, wait a minute," said Delfina, offended by Damy's brusqueness. "*Míralo, qué grosero.*"

"Conde, where the hell have you been? Sure. Sure. That's O.K. Never mind. Conde, mah man. Guess what I got here in neat little tight packets? Yep. You got it. Never fear when Damy's here. And guess, just guess who picked it up for us? No. Nope. Close but no cigar. You're going to crack up. It was your fruitcake aunt. Yeah. Isn't that a stitch? Man, you were right. She doesn't have both oars in the water. Get this, she thinks I'm the . . .

"Of course. You'll get your cut. You'll get it when you come get me out of this hole. You haven't exactly been overwhelming me with get-well calls and visits. Yeah, I know you're hot. I don't care. I just want to get out of here. When? *Now.* Right now. I don't give a shit. Just come get me out of here. It's pitch-black out and we can do it. To use your phrase, 'Trust me, my fren.' Good. Besides, 'No tickee, no shirtee.' Let me put it in a way you'll understand. Either you get me out or you lose your share. Think it over. I thought you'd see it my way. Good boy. O.K., do what you have to do and then pick me up right after that. I'm going bug-fuck here. Thata-boy."

Damy kept staring at the receiver after hanging up.

"*¿Qué pasa?*"

"Yeah. What?"

"What is up?"

"Conde's coming here to pick me up."

"When?"

"In about half an hour."

"Conde is coming? Here?"

Delfina was stunned. Her *ratero* nephew would try to get her car. The minute he found out she owned a car, he would try to get it from her. If you had a little something, a little bundle, Conde and his *ratero* friends always wanted it. They were like *zopilotes.* Vultures. He would *not* get her car. She had sacrificed too much for it. For openers she had just sold her immortal soul for all eternity. She had to do something. But what? Delfina panicked. *Sinvergüenza.* He was *not* going to take the car. She had already paid a dollar for it. She had to do something.

Damy went over to the sofa to sit down. "God, it's going to be nice getting out of here. 'Waiter, a steak, medium well, please. Also a pizza: pepperoni and Italian sausage. There you are, my good man, and keep the change.'"

"Those things are not good for you. You should have some *pozole.*"

"And Rita. Oh, baby, stand by," said Damy, running a hand through his greasy hair. "She'll think I've been at sea for two years." Thinking of Rita, Damy leaned back, looked up at the ceiling and folded his hands behind his head. "Cripes, do I stink." Damy sniffed at himself. "I've *got* to take a shower."

"A bath."

"A shower."

"Good luck. A bath."

"A bath? You mean to tell me you don't even have a shower?"

"A bath takes less water and we should save the water."

"Hell, a bath takes forever. But, Jesus, I *need* one." Facetiously, Damy asked, "You don't happen to have a pair of men's shorts on you, by any chance, do you?"

"Yep."

"You *do?*"

"Yes. They belonged to Panchito, my ex-husband. I was keeping them in the trunk for *momentos.* But, *ya que, todo cambia,* everything changes. What do I need them for anymore? They are like new. A little big for you. But it's O.K."

Damy shook his head. "No kidding. Are they clean?"

"Of course they are clean."

"How about a man's shirt? You don't happen to have one of those back there in your pile of 'momentos.'"

"I got one in the trunk too." Damy threw his head back and laughed. "What is so funny?" Damy shook his head. "I will get them for you."

It was while she was getting the clothing out of an old stand-up trunk and then running Damy's bathwater that Delfina's strategic master plan began to gel. She held Benjie and whispered in his ear, "We will do it, Benjie." On her knees, by the bathtub, Delfina clenched her fists and made a vow. "That *ratero* Conde will not take my car, that *maldito sinvergüenza* will not take my car. It belongs to me." She called out to Damy. *"Oiga, yoo-hoo-le,* your water is running! There is some champoo here and some soap and the clothes are here on the toilet."

Damy peeked into the bathroom. "How about a towel?"

"Over there."

"O.K., well, I'll need some privacy."

Delfina smiled. "What for? I already know what you look like. You cannot chock me."

"Beat it."

Picking up Benjie, Delfina whispered, "My pleasure, *Demonio. A Dios.* It has been nice knowing you."


The song blasted out:

"Oh-oh, Lo-o-ordy, Geordie, make the Goo-ood Times roll, pray-ay-sed by they ho-oh, owa holy name, Gee-oh-ho-ho-hordy. Shee-ee-eet . . ." Delfina had just turned on the car radio. She pushed another button, changing stations, to hear "Get on dow-own, momma; get on dow-own, momma;

get on dow-won, momma, you can make it feel so good. Baby, baby, bay-ay-ay-ay-bee . . .''

Devil music, thought Delfina, as she switched off the radio. But that was O.K. When you got a car from the Devil you had to listen to it. That was probably the only kind of music the car could play.

The wind felt good on Delfina's face. She was in her car and was racing west on Freeway 280, beneath a San Francisco moon. With Benjie in the passenger's seat, Delfina felt free. It was a wonderful feeling; it was a wonderful car even if it wasn't a *Cadiyác*. But a *Cheeby* was O.K. too. *Algo es mejor que nada,* she thought. Something is better than nothing. Delfina was exhilarated.

Delfina looked at Benjie and smiled at her unbelievable coup. "We did it, *precioso*. We did it. You helped me."

While the water was still running for Damy Taggart's bath, she had tiptoed out of the house with a sweater and Benjie in one hand and the car keys, her purse and the certificate of title in the other. She had carefully opened the garage door and eased the vehicle out of the garage and into the night.

Delfina sighed as she sped along the freeway. "Nothing will ever spoil our happiness again, Benjie," she said just as a flashing light reflected in her rearview mirror.

"¡*Aiii, Chihuahua!*" Delfina adjusted the mirror and sped up. The flashing light pursued her for a mile and then was accompanied by the sound of a siren. The light and siren would not go away. A California Highway Patrol officer on a motorcycle came alongside of her and pointed a gloved hand at Delfina and then to the side of the road.

"*Aiii, Dios mío, qué relajo.* I think that means we have to stop, Benjie," said Delfina as she brought the car to an abrupt, dusty halt on the shoulder of the road.

The patrolman, holding a large flashlight, stepped up to the car.

"My name is Sergeant Torres. Would you mind stepping out of the car?"

"Ah, Torres, that is the name of my brother's wife and her family in Modesto. Are you from Modesto, Torres?"

"No, ma'am. I'm from Walnut Creek."

"Do you have any cousins or family in Modesto?"

"No, ma'am, I don't. Ma'am, I'm going to have to ask you to step out of the car."

"What for?"

"Ma'am, you were clocked traveling in excess of ninety miles an hour."

Delfina got out of the car holding her purse in one hand. *"¡Ni lo mande la Santa Virgen!"* exclaimed Delfina. "Benjie, you stay here to watch my car." Sergeant Torres towered over Delfina. *"Hijo.* For a Mexican you are a big guy. *¿Sabes?* I bet you must have big dinners."

"Hold on." Torres received a message on his helmet earphones and spoke into a small microphone an inch from his lips.

Delfina was impressed. *"Ah, mira. Qué* tricky. I thought you were talking to me."

"Ma'am, do you know you're driving a car with stolen plates?"

"What plates? I never stole plates. In my kitchen I have all the plates I need."

"Whose car is this?"

"Mine."

"May I see the registration?"

"Of course," said Delfina, proudly plucking a green document from her purse.

Sergeant Torres took the paper and studied it by the light of a flashlight. "This isn't the registration. This is the certificate of title. Is this your current address?"

"Yep."

"You bought this car today from Damien Taggart?"

"No, I bought it from *El Demonio.*"

"But it says Damien Taggart here on this certificate. Ma'am, this car has been involved in the killing of a policeman. Did you know that?"

"*¡Ni lo mande la Santa Virgen!*"

"Do you know the owner?"

"Chure. Me. I just told you. *No seas cabezón.* I am the owner of the car. I paid a dollar for it. Well, not really a dollar. *¿Sabes?* It was like four quarters."

"Who did you buy it from?"

"*El Demonio.*"

"You mean Damien Taggart."

"No, I mean *El Demonio.* He got big wound right here" —Delfina indicated the right side of her body—"that St. Michael the Archangel gave him in the fight. I gave him *pozole* and *albóndiga* soups."

"When did you last see him?"

"St. Michael the Archangel?"

"No, Damien Taggart."

"*El Demonio.* Just now. He was going to take a bath."

"When, exactly, did you last see him?"

"*A ver . . .*" Delfina pulled back her left sleeve to let Sergeant Torres see her pretty pink Swatch watch. "Just . . .

*Mira. A ver.*" Delfina counted on her fingers. "Ten minutes ago."

"He's at your house? Now? At 850 Ortigalita?"

"Yep. He is waiting for my nephew, the *ratero,* to pick him up."

"Who's that?"

"Conde Pacheco."

Sergeant Torres walked toward his motorcycle as he spoke into his microphone mentioning Damy Taggart and Conde Pacheco and reading Delfina's address from the certificate of title. When he returned to Delfina she had already gotten into the car, where she was holding Benjie in her arms.

"I'm afraid you're going to have to follow me, ma'am."

"Ah, *sí?* Where are we going?"

"Some people are very interested in talking to you."

"Ah, *sí?*" Delfina was flattered.


Delfina followed the patrolman to the Mission District CHP station at Ninth and Army streets, where the car was impounded and she was subjected to an exhaustive interrogation —exhaustive to the police interrogators, not to Delfina, who thoroughly enjoyed all the attention.

Afterwards, Delfina was ushered into a drab waiting room outfitted with two rows of molded-plastic chairs and a battered television set tuned to a late-night sports program. Before she sat down, Delfina walked over to the TV set.

"Maybe they have an old movie with Pedro Armendariz or Dolores Del Rio, Benjie," she said as she rapidly turned the channel selector. "It's too late for the *telenovelas.*" She paused on one of the channels. *"Mira,* Benjie, what a cute little house. It almost looks like ours, *verdad?*"

Delfina switched channels until she came to a Spanish-language station that was showing an old movie starring Cantinflas, the great Mexican comedian.

"*Hijo,* Benjie, Cantinflas!" said Delfina as she settled into a chair with the cat on her lap.

What Delfina missed on three local channels was the assault by police on her Ortigalita Street home. Had she watched, she would have seen Conde Pacheco tramping out of her house with his hands in the air and, a short while later, a shot being fired from inside the house.

As Delfina dozed to the antics of Cantinflas, the San Francisco police and a SWAT team responded to Damy Taggart's shot by emptying their weapons, tear gas and smoke grenades into her compact home.

Early the next morning Delfina was allowed to inspect her home, which was surrounded by yellow police barrier tape and a few spectators. She was appalled by what she saw: All of the walls of her living room were pocked with bullet holes. The windows were broken. Her television set was destroyed. There was blood splattered across the living room floor. Photographs of her late husband and brother were destroyed. Her pictures of John F. Kennedy and the Sacred Heart of Jesus had been shredded into cat litter. Her sofa was ripped beyond recognition.

Delfina sighed, and then began to call for Benjie, who had dashed away, frightened by the sights and smells in the wrecked house.

"Benjie? Where are you, *gatito,* come here, my baby." Delfina searched the house frantically, but Benjie was nowhere to be found. She sat on a broken chair and began to cry. "Now

I have even lost my Benjie," she wept, picking up the shredded picture of Panchito. "Everything is destroyed, everything is gone . . ."

But before she could finish, Benjie appeared magically, expertly sidestepping the wreckage and rubbing himself against her ankles.

"*Aiii,* you scared me. Where were you, you naughty boy?"

She picked up the overweight cat and hugged it as tears ran down her cheeks. "Out looking for your girl friend again? I know you, *parrandero.* Looks like they had a big party right here, *verdad?*"

The cat purred contentedly in her arms, closing its eyes and tightening its claws as Delfina rubbed its stomach.

Just then a television news crew arrived on the scene.

# Las Señoritas Lucrecia y Dolores

**"S**o many things have happened," said Senorita Lucrecia.
"Too many things," said Senorita Dolores.

# 31. The Cortege

"So many things have happened," said Señorita Lucrecia.

"Too many things," said Señorita Dolores.

"Maybe there will be nothing more to talk about."

"*Aiii,* don't say that, *querida.* There will always be *something* to talk about."

"You are right. *Gracias a Dios.* There will *always* be something to talk about. *Aiii, mira,* look at the time. Well, I've got to go now, dear. I have so many things to do."

"Yes, I know. Where does the time go?"

"*¿Quién sabe?*"

"Be sure to cover up. It's cold outside."

"I will."

"Here. Let me get your shawl, *querida.*"

"*Gracias.*"

"Take care of yourself, Lucrecia."

"You too, Dolores."

Señorita Lucrecia adjusted a black shawl across her shoulders as she bid farewell to her good friend. Before she parted she turned for one final comment. "Don't you think it was so beautiful?"

"It was wonderful."

"It really *was* wonderful. That is the only word that can possibly describe it."

"*A Dios,* Lucrecia."
"*A Dios,* Dolores."

What Señorita Lucrecia and Señorita Dolores were describing was not the ceremony but the procession of cars for the wedding of Shark Salazar and Celine Caballos.

A presidential motorcade or a parade of military liberators entering a bombed and defeated country could not have been as impressive.

Shark had rented a white stretch limousine which was festooned with strings of white paper flowers. The automobile had a bar, a television set, a telephone and a vase filled with fresh carnations. The car came complete with a Mexican chauffeur who kept throwing his head back and sniffing from an inhaler. *"Pinchi* allergies are killing me, *ese.* My cousin says I should move with him to Scottsdale, Arizona, where I could breathe."

All of the other cars—twenty in all—were decorated with yellow paper flowers. The best man drove a pink El Dorado Cadillac convertible and behind that came a candy-apple-red Mustang that was slung so low to the ground that a small rock would have scraped its underside. Rows of dingle balls hung above the inside of the windshield. ("Low and slow, baby. It's a real cherry.")

Behind the Mustang was a customized pickup truck that was bright yellow. The front part of the truck had been painted red, making it appear as if bright flames were emerging from the engine. The windshield consisted of two small glass slits that made driving extremely hazardous. It would not be the first or last time safety would be sacrificed for style.

Manny Caballos drove his Oldsmobile just ahead of a

large flatbed truck driven by the bride's brother, Carlos Caballos. It too was decorated with strings of paper flowers. Carlos had not bothered to cover the new signs on the sides of the truck which now proudly proclaimed, "Caballos & Salazar."

Behind that came a faded Buick with a dented fender and a taped, broken window. Nobody knew who the occupants were. Shark's family came in a camper. From an upper window in the camper a little girl could be seen giggling. Various Fords and Chevrolets followed.

Many of the cars had a variety of items hanging from rearview mirrors: rosaries, religious medals, knit angora dice, a picture of *La Virgen de Guadalupe,* photographs of children in gold lockets, high school mortarboard tassels.

And bringing up the rear was Delfina Varela, driving her Corvette, the one she kept insisting was given to her by the Devil. Sitting beside her, on a cardboard box placed on the passenger seat, was Benjie. A deodorizer shaped like a pine tree hung from the rearview mirror. Delfina looked proud and very happy. The only thing missing was Anthony Quinn and a bright sailboat-motif Hermes scarf to proclaim her triumph.

After the wedding, the bride and bridesmaids filled the cars with their elaborate chiffon and lace dresses, which billowed out like gigantic matilija poppies. From inside the white limousine, the radiant bride and her stalwart groom waved regally to others standing outside the church. Celine looked at Shark affectionately. She studied the terrible scar on his face. That night, her small breasts bathed in moonlight, she would run a finger along the length of the scar and whisper, "Oh Shark," a sigh that would blend with the low moan of a ship's horn echoing across the San Francisco Bay.

And then, in a neat straight line, the cars, their horns

rejoicing, departed the church in a harmonic exaltation to the promise of matrimony.

The cortege pulled away from the Basilica of Mission Dolores and drove past Mission Dolores Park and Mission High School. In the background could be seen the statue of Miguel Hidalgo, "Libertador de México, 1810," as pigeons continued their inexorable desecration of the great emancipator by defecating on the statue's nose.

A motorcycle roared by. Riding the motorcycle was a fat man with a red beard wearing a black World War II German helmet. On the helmet, in white lettering, were the words "Death Before Dishonor." The rider, who waved at the wedding party, was leaning so far back in his seat he could barely reach the handlebars.

The cortege passed a number of iron grates guarding sidewalk doors and windows as a young, dark woman ran by wearing a brown dress, a white apron and shower slippers. Two men sitting on a front stoop eyed the woman's brown, hairy legs as she ran by, her shower slippers flapping, her pigtail swinging.

The wedding party passed a mural of a waterfall, mountains, clouds and a Mayan jungle filled with green pyramids. The mural covered the entire front wall of the Community Law Building that also housed the Real Good Karma Natural Food Restaurant.

Celine smiled at the sight of graffiti that proclaimed, "Chiquita Loves Shorty," as the sights, sounds and smells of La Michon began to create a sensual mirage.

At a curb a man was selling plaster saints, blankets and T-shirts from the back of a Chevrolet pickup truck. One of the

T-shirts displayed a modified version of the Coca-Cola logo that read *"Coma Caca."*

The Transfer Club marquee announced, "Music and Disco, 9 P.M. until 5 A.M., Fri., Sat., Sun. Live Music & Disco. Orquesta Ciencia Latina."

The automobiles drove along Twenty-second Street past a row of businesses that included Diane's Health Food, Lilly's Beauty Salon, and Palm and Psychic Readings by Angela. In an upstairs apartment a pink teddy bear was wedged in a window, propping it open.

Painted across the front of Cesar's Dance Hall were several silver stars and the names Mongo Santamaria, Las Hermanas Silva, Alberto Santiago, Las Estrellas de Colombia, Johnny Nelson, Orquesta Sensual, Jose Fajardo, Joe Cuba, Tito Puentes, Monique, Charanga 76, Hector La Vae, Larry Harlow, Bobby Rodriguez, Willi BoBo, Machito and Ray Barreto.

And, finally, before dropping out of sight, the cortege passed a massive sign advertising one of the District's premier businesses—Sandoval's Multi-Services: Insurance (Auto, Truck, Life, Home, Commercial); Legal (Eulalio V. Palacios, Attorney, civil/criminal); Matrimonios; Taxes; Immigration; Naturalization; Adopciones; Divorcios; Funcrarios. Shark Salazar pointed to the sign and Celine smiled. The services seemed to embody the entire cycle of existence; above all the totality and futility of life in *La Michon.*

# About the Author

Louie García Robinson was born in El Paso, Texas, and grew up in East Los Angeles. The former head of national communications for the Mexican American Political Association, Robinson has worked in public relations and as a magazine editor and newspaper reporter. He lives in San Francisco, where he is at work on a new novel.